HEROES
ON
HORSEBACK

HEROES ON HORSEBACK

the story of the PONY EXPRESS

by TOM WEST

Blackie: London and Glasgow

First published in Great Britain in 1972
by Blackie & Son Limited
5 Fitzhardinge Street, London W1H 0DL.
Bishopbriggs, Glasgow G64 2NZ

ISBN 0 216 89335 6

Printed in Great Britain by R. & R. Clark Ltd, Edinburgh

ACKNOWLEDGMENTS

For reprint permission, grateful acknowledgment is made to:
The Bettmann Archive: pp. 14, 30
Brown Brothers: p. 73
Chamber of Commerce, Gothenburg, Nebraska: p. 36
History Room, Wells Fargo Bank, San Francisco: pp. 13, 56-7
Kansas State Historical Society: p. 107
Nebraska State Historical Society: p. 98
State Historical Society of Colorado: p. 98
St. Joseph Museum, St. Joseph, Missouri: pp. 123, 153

CONTENTS

1

The Mail Must Go Through

Bob Haslam stood in the shade of the lonely rock-and-adobe relay station known as Friday's, set on the Nevada plains and surrounded by a sea of gray-green sage.

Bob was young, wiry, and tough as rawhide—a typical Pony Express rider. His saddle horse was tied close by. It was a fine animal, with long deep barrel and muscular shoulders, and it could outrun any Indian pony. The Pony Express used only the best.

Bob was bow-legged, like a cowboy, but although he was still in his teens, he considered himself just a little bit better than a cowboy. Born on a ranch, he had been riding a pony ever since he could walk, and he was an expert horseman. Bob was one of eighty riders, carefully chosen from hundreds of applicants, who were posted across the United States, from St. Joseph, Missouri, to San Francisco. At each relay station they waited, poised. Their job was to rush the *mochila* to the next station. In all, they covered a span of 1,966 miles, most of it wild, desolate country—flaming desert, vast prairies, rugged mountains. There was always danger from rampaging Indians, renegades, swollen rivers, blizzards. But the schedule allowed only ten days to cover the entire route, and to maintain this schedule, the *mochila* had to travel two hundred miles every day. This meant every rider must travel at breakneck speed, switching the *mochila* to a fresh pony every twelve to fifteen miles.

Nothing stopped these daring riders—*the mail had to go through.* Sometimes a rider limped in with an arrow protruding from his back, as did one Mexican. Others collapsed over their ponies' withers, drilled by a renegade bullet, as did Bob Walker. Yet their code was inflexible: the mail came first, the horse second, the rider last.

It was not surprising that Bob Haslam was proud to be a rider for the Pony Express.

Every now and then Bob's anxious gaze swept the horizon, where black smudges of smoke told of burning homesteads. It was spring, 1861, and the Paiute Indians were "out"—on the warpath—sacking and killing throughout Nevada. At other Pony Express stations stock tenders had been murdered, the stations ransacked, the saddle stock run off. Death was ever-present. But Bob wasn't worried about Paiutes. His mind was on the *mochila,*

The *mochila*.

containing the mail, which was overdue. He wondered if Tom Kelly, the Express rider who was supposed to deliver it to him, so that he could rush it to the next relay station, had been killed.

Nothing was quite like the *mochila*, he thought. It was specially designed for the purpose of carrying mail, and consisted of a square leather sheet which was thrown over the saddle, covering it completely. The saddle horn and cantle protruded through slits. A leather box, known as a *cantina*, was sewn into each corner. The four *cantinas* contained the mail and were locked.

The rider sat on the *mochila* so that the mail could not be lost. The four *cantinas* in the corners distributed the weight evenly on the pony. If the rider were thrown or wounded, the *mochila* would remain in place and would be carried to the next station by the riderless pony. It could be switched from one mount to another in a flash—the rider simply stepped out of the saddle, lifted the *mochila* off and flopped it across his fresh mount. There

Changing horses at an
Express station.
were no straps to unbuckle, no leather whangs to untie. The
complete transfer from horse to horse took less than two minutes.

Bob Haslam's run was to the station known as Buckland's, across
terrain swarming with the deadly Paiutes. The last rider from
the west had reported seeing a stagecoach near Cold Creek, gutted
and still smoking, with the dead bodies of its passengers lying
nearby. Young Haslam would be riding over this trail, but he
wasn't worried. He just wasn't the worrying kind.

A stock tender walked up. "Tom Kelly's overdue," he said
gloomily. "Maybe the redskins killed him."

"You guessed wrong, Jack," smiled Haslam, gazing across the
glaring flats. "He's coming!"

A dust plume rose above the vast expanse of sage, gradually
creeping closer. Soon Haslam and the stock tender saw a rider,
frantically spurring.

Kelly came in like a cyclone, and flung himself out of the saddle.
His pony stood, head lowered, plastered with sweat. Haslam ran
toward him, grabbed the *mochila,* and swung it across his own
saddle.

"Gosh!" gasped Kelly. "I sure scraped through at Tumbling
Rock. Injuns as thick as fleas. 'Most lifted my scalp."

"Maybe you better stick around, Bob," suggested a stock tender.
"I'd say you got no more chance of reaching Smith's Creek than
reaching the moon."

Haslam, who never allowed himself more than one minute for
a "switch-over," vaulted onto his pony even before the man had
finished speaking. "So-long!" he yelled, and raised the reins. The
dun's plunging hooves scattered dust and pebbles. He shot off
like a rocket.

Haslam carried no rifle, to save weight. Two Colt revolving pistols were stuck under his belt.

At first everything went well. In quick succession he traded ponies at three relay stations—Mount Airy, Castle Rock and Cold Springs—without a sign of an Indian. Then a setback came at Reese River station. There wasn't a horse or a mule on the place. All the animals had been taken to mount men, who were chasing a ravaging band of Indians. No pony, however willing, could be expected to hold a fast pace for more than fifteen miles, but Haslam had no option. He watered his weary horse, climbed into the saddle and pressed on.

He nursed the tired pony another fifteen miles to Bucklands, the next station. Here he would find a relief rider and could rest his own weary bones. He had been in the saddle for almost a hundred miles.

To his surprise, there was no relief standing ready at Bucklands to grab the precious *mochila*. He swung out of the saddle and hurried into the station. The station keeper and his helper were playing cards at a plank table. Hunched on a chair, nervously smoking a cigarette, was the relief rider, a substitute, hastily hired. The Pony Express was shorthanded.

"Say, aren't you riding?" demanded Haslam.

"No, I'm sick," answered the other sourly.

"He's yellow, scared of Injuns," declared the station keeper.

Haslam wasted no time on the man. "I'll ride for him," he snapped. "Give me a horse, a good one. Hurry!"

Astride a fresh horse, he rode out, squinting into the setting sun. Three more quick changes, he thought, and he'd be on the last lap, Smith's Creek. He was tired out. His every limb seemed to be weighted with lead, and every bone in his body ached. Jay

Kelley was due to take over at Smith's Creek. He could depend upon Jay. Then he would be able to lie down and sleep. Sleep! He'd never craved it more.

Drugged with fatigue, he failed to notice the bay's ears flip up with alarm. The pony was racing through a shallow bowl, carpeted with sage and squatty greasewood. High-pitched yells suddenly shattered the brooding quiet. On either side feathered heads bobbed up out of the brush.

Haslam dropped low over his pony and urged it to greater speed. Its hooves drummed over the sun-baked ground. Arrows droned through the air, and guns flashed and thundered. Head outstretched, wind whistling through its nostrils, the bay leaped through the brush, and in seconds a mob of painted warriors was left behind. Haslam sighed with relief and straightened in the saddle but quickly dropped down again when bullets whined past his head. He glanced backward. A dozen or more mounted braves were on his trail. Crouched low, he urged the bay on.

Again he looked back. The Paiutes were beginning to string out, and many were lagging behind. Four, however, in a bunch, were not more than fifty paces behind, and they were gaining on him.

For a moment, Haslam was puzzled. He knew no Indian pony could keep pace with the Express Company's carefully selected mounts. Then he remembered the stations that had been raided and burned all along the line. The Paiutes were riding stolen Express ponies!

Now he could hear the steady drum of hooves, drawing closer, closer. The bay, its muzzle foam-flecked, was tiring. He grabbed the butt of one of the Colt pistols tucked under his belt, swung around and fired three times into the dark block of Indians.

One pony plunged down in a flurry of dust. Another rose high, forelegs flailing. Guns spouted lead in return. Stabbing pain bit into Haslam's gun-arm. His hand was numb. The smoking gun slipped from his fingers and was lost. Useless, the injured arm dangled by his side.

He dropped the reins and snapped out the remaining gun with his left hand. Again he twisted around in the saddle and fired. Two Indians still pounded behind him, little more than a pony's length away.

The leading horse and rider crashed down. Close behind them, the lone remaining Paiute jerked his mount to a stop, a Winchester rifle gripped in one hand. He levelled the gun and fired.

The bullet ripped through Haslam's cheek, knocked out a whole row of teeth, and smashed the jawbone. Stunned, blood-soaked from the two wounds, he sagged over the saddle horn, fighting to keep his seat. Somehow, (he could never remember just how) he managed to throw off his pursuer and escape. When his senses finally cleared, he found himself riding into a relay station. Two stock tenders stood gaping at his bloodied form.

"You're in no shape to ride," insisted one. "Bill or me will take the *mochila* on."

Haslam eyed the men. Both were too heavy for fast riding. "Get me a horse," he mumbled, "I'm going through."

Remounted, he rode on. A strip of towel was stuffed into his mouth to staunch the bleeding. The remainder of the towel was wrapped around his gashed right forearm.

By a miracle of endurance he reached Smith's Creek and turned the *mochila* over to Jay Kelley. He had covered 185 miles.

He sank into deep sleep while they were patching up his wounds. It seemed he had scarcely closed his eyes when the station tender shook him awake. The rider heading east had just ridden in, barely able to sit the saddle. His right leg was broken.

"His pony threw him," explained the station tender. "Thought you'd like to know, Bob. Guess he stays here, and his *mochila*."

"He stays, but not the *mochila*," insisted Haslam in a hoarse whisper. His right arm, bandaged, was stiffening. "That mail's got to go through," he said stubbornly. "I'm riding!"

And ride he did! Half dead from fatigue, badly crippled, he hauled himself up on a horse and headed out with the *mochila*, retracing the trail over which he had recently travelled.

It was quite dark now and the stars shone brightly overhead.

Too pain-ridden and weary to care about Indians, Haslam hurtled through the night. At Cold Springs, where he had changed mounts riding out, he found nothing but smoking embers and the bodies of two dead men, bristling with arrows. Twice the Paiutes chased him. More dead than alive, he finally dragged himself into Friday's, his home station. Tom Kelly was waiting. He grabbed the *mochila* and sped eastward. The stock tenders carried Bob Haslam into the station, for he was too weak to stand.

Young Bob Haslam had ridden 370 miles in thirty-six hours, without a pause except for one short break, and despite two bullet wounds, either of which would have stopped many men.

Two comparisons will reveal the extent of his accomplishment. A troop of United States cavalry covers thirty miles in a day's march. Fifty miles is considered the limit. Alexander the Great's cavalry, the swiftest in the ancient world, could ride seventy miles in a day.

The Express Company awarded Haslam $100 in recognition of his feat. Bob thought it was nothing to get fussed up about. He was a Pony Express rider. Wasn't it his job?

2

The Great Hunger

What brought the Pony Express into existence? Hunger for news.

East and West were not connected, as they are today, by jet plane service, railroads, highways, telegraph, and telephone. Almost two thousand miles of wild terrain and roaming bands of hostile Indians lay between them. There were only two means by which a person in the East could send a message to a friend or relative in the West: first, he could entrust it to someone in a wagon train heading west. The wagon train might, or might not, reach California, and it would take many months to cross the vast plains. Second, he could locate a ship sailing for San Francisco, via Cape Horn, a voyage which also took months.

But on January 24, 1848, James Marshall found a gold nugget in the mill race of Sutter's Mill, California. That discovery started the greatest stampede in history. Almost everyone in California rushed into the Sierra foothills in a frantic search for gold. In a few days Yerba Buena (San Francisco) was a ghost town, and so were other California towns—Sonoma, San Jose, Santa Cruz, Monterey. Soldiers deserted their posts, sailors abandoned their ships and workers quit their jobs.

Almost *six months* passed before the news of the gold discovery reached the eastern states. Then every town and hamlet resounded with the news, "Gold! Gold in California!" It is said that the bearded miner who brought the tidings from California stepped into a New York barber shop to have his beard shaved off. The barber carefully washed the severed whiskers in a basin of water—and panned enough gold dust to buy his wife a new watch. Many such yarns circulated and were believed, and another far greater rush ensued. Everyone, it seemed, was headed for California. The gold-crazed hordes came by wagon across the Great Plains, by ship around Cape Horn, by muleback across the Isthmus of Panama. For two months, a continuous caravan of white-topped wagons, like a gigantic centipede, crept across the plains between Missouri and Fort Laramie.

Gold fever even swept the world.

Eager for wealth, men poured into California from Europe, South America, Australia. Quickly, the "land of gold" teemed with immigrants. Within five years their number increased to half a million.

Soon, these adventurers began to crave one thing even more than gold. They wanted news from home—letters from their wives, sweethearts, parents, children; newspapers telling what was happening in the outside world.

There were no letters or newspapers, and the demand for mail service grew thunderous.

A petition, signed by 75,000 Californians, was sent to Congress in Washington, D.C. Thousands of anxious women in the East, awaiting word from husbands who had gone to California to seek fortunes, pestered the politicians. Those harried politicians did their best. They made hasty contracts with freighting outfits and stage lines to carry mail across the prairies. All these attempts to cross the plains ended in failure, however, for the distance was too far, and the obstacles too great.

In desperation, the Government turned to sea transport. The Pacific Mail Steamship Company agreed to carry mail from New York to San Francisco, once a month. For this the Government would pay a subsidy of $199,000 a year.

The first vessel to carry mail, the *California,* took over four months to make the 15,000-mile voyage around Cape Horn. No sooner had she dropped her anchor in San Francisco Bay than the entire crew deserted and rushed to the gold fields. The *California* joined the huge fleet of abandoned vessels whose masts made a forlorn forest in the Bay.

But the Pacific Mail maintained its service. Whenever one of its side-wheelers churned through the Golden Gate, at the entrance to San Francisco's harbor, a semaphore on Telegraph Hill broadcast the news. Bearded miners, frock-coated gamblers, red-shirted teamsters, soberly-clad traders rushed to the Post Office. The long line of men eagerly seeking letters extended for blocks through the teeming tent city. Often they stood in line all day and through the night. Men charged $20 to hold a place. The two or three clerks inside the Post Office were literally buried beneath an avalanche of letters and parcels.

When, after endless hours of slowly shuffling forward, a man finally reached the lone wicket, his letter—if he were lucky enough to receive one—was at least four months old.

What became of mail addressed to the thousands of men living in Sierra City, Michigan Bluff, Chinese Camp, Murphy's, Ben Hur, Timbuctoo, and the other tent towns of Northern California? The letters gathered dust in San Francisco, for California had only one Post Office and no delivery service.

One alert young man solved the problem with his "Jackass Mail." Alexander H. Todd was a shrewd young fellow who grew tired of standing in line, with the dank Bay fog biting into his bones. He stepped around to the back door of the Post Office and peered inside. Stack upon stack of mail bags were jammed into the barnlike room, and a few shirt-sleeved postal clerks were wrestling hopelessly with mountains of mail.

"Can I lend a hand?" inquired Todd.

"We could use a hundred pairs of hands," the harried postmaster told him.

Todd took off his coat and went to work. Maybe, he thought, he'd find his own mail. As he worked, an idea came to him.

The following day he boarded a steamer for Sacramento and the mining camps. His first call was Dutch Flat, scene of a "strike." He stepped into the nearest shanty saloon, which was packed with ragged miners. Rapping on the counter to get attention, he raised his voice. "Boys," he shouted, "there's mountains of letters stacked up in San Francisco. Any man who wants his mail give me a dollar.

I'll dig it out. When I deliver I expect an ounce of gold dust."

Todd was swamped with a flood of orders. He hurried back to San Francisco, persuaded the postmaster to swear him in as an extra clerk—without pay—and searched for his customers' mail.

He found so much that he had to buy a jackass to pack it up to Dutch Flat. He also picked up all the old newspapers he could find. They brought $8 apiece at the mining camps.

Thus the "Jackass Mail" was born.

Meanwhile Washington, D.C., was flooded with complaints. Steamship mail service was too slow. Six to nine months seemed like a lifetime to wait for a reply to a letter sent east.

To stifle the outcry, Congress tried to speed up the mail. A railroad was constructed across the fever-ridden Isthmus of Panama, to shorten the voyage around the Horn. Camels were even imported from the Sahara Desert. It was hoped that they would carry the mail across the southern deserts. The experiment failed.

Congress finally decided that the only practical method of providing mail service to the West was an overland route, using sturdy stagecoaches. It offered an annual subsidy of $600,000 to anyone who would guarantee to provide semi-weekly service.

John Butterfield, a well-known stagecoach operator, won the contract. He was backed by four great express companies—Adams, American, National, and Wells, Fargo.

The selected route was known as the "Oxbow." Looping through the southern states, it was 760 miles longer than the northern immigrant route, but it avoided the tortuous passes of the Sierra Nevada and the sub-zero winters of the northern plains. What it couldn't avoid were the savage Comanches and Apaches who roved the Southwest.

Butterfield hired 800 men and set them to work building stage stations every twenty miles along the route. They labored a year to complete the buildings. Then Butterfield bought 100 new Concord coaches and 1,000 mules to haul them. He installed station keepers and stock hands in the newly-built stations, then freighted supplies to them by wagon.

On September 15, 1858, the first coach left St. Louis for the coast. Another pulled out of San Francisco that same day heading east. Butterfield had contracted to deliver mail in twenty-five days.

But California, now pouring millions in gold into the coffers of the East, was not satisfied. It still took a month for a letter to arrive. Senator Gwin of California fought hard for a northern route. The Oxbow route, he declared, was slow, uncertain and wasteful. Many Butterfield stages were being attacked by Comanche, Kiowa and Apache. The Indians burned the coaches, murdered the passengers, scattered the mail.

But Butterfield's bright-red coaches continued to bump along, crawling over desert and mountain. Sometimes they made ten miles an hour, more often five. At times they were held up for days by Indian raids or swollen rivers.

Then another gold rush thrilled the nation. The yellow metal had been discovered in Colorado. Immigrant trains again streamed across the plains and this time the slogan was, "Pike's Peak or Bust."

Boom towns blossomed. A renewed chorus of complaint arose when their citizens had to wait six weeks to receive a letter from the East. Why, indignant westerners demanded, did their mail have to travel halfway around the globe?

The West needed a northern route, thundered Senator Gwin,

a route 760 miles shorter. His fellow senators were unmoved. President Buchanan had strong Southern sympathies. Aaron V. Brown, Postmaster General, was a Southerner, too, and he had selected the "Oxbow" route.

One day an unexpected visitor strode into Senator Gwin's office in Washington, D.C. "My name is Russell," he said crisply. "I am a partner in the freighting firm of Russell, Majors and Waddell. I can get your mail from east to west in ten days."

The senator stared, unbelieving. If he hadn't known that Russell, Majors and Waddell was one of the biggest freighting outfits in the country, he would have laughed. The claim seemed ridiculous.

"Indeed, Mr. Russell," he said politely. "How on earth do you propose to do it?"

"Fast ponies!"

"Ponies!" smiled the senator. "Over a two thousand-mile route?"

"Why not?" retorted Russell. "Wells, Fargo beat a steamship to Portland, Oregon, with relays of riders from San Francisco. That's over a thousand miles. Give me a government contract and we'll cut Butterfield's time in half, in less than half. Look! I have the route sketched out."

He laid a map of the United States on the senator's desk. A black line had been inked across it, linking St. Joseph, Missouri, with San Francisco. Unlike the looping southern route, the line cut straight from east to west. At regular intervals it was dotted.

"Those dots," explained Russell, "are relay stations, spaced fifteen miles apart. My riders will travel at full gallop and switch ponies at every station. One man can easily cover a seventy-five-mile span."

"A pony express!" murmured Gwin. "It sounds fantastic."

"Two hundred miles a day!" continued Russell. "Four days to Salt Lake City, then another six days to San Francisco." His voice rose with enthusiasm. "It can be done! We'll use the fastest horses and finest riders in the West."

"How much time would be required to launch this project?"

"Give me sixty-five days," returned Russell promptly, then added, "Now how about that government subsidy?"

"H'm!" Gwin fingered his chin. "It doesn't seem feasible. Congress will need to be convinced. They'll have to be shown."

"I'll show them!"

"Splendid!" smiled the senator. "Just prove that the idea is practical. I'll do the rest."

He knew that Russell, Majors and Waddell were reputed to own over 6,000 freight wagons and 75,000 freight oxen. Over 5,000 bullwhackers, blacksmiths, and laborers were on their payroll. They already had a government contract to carry mail on their stage line from Leavenworth, Kansas, to Salt Lake City.

Russell, however, had to convince his partners, who knew nothing about his plan. That, he knew, would be difficult. They were freighters and hardheaded business men. They thought in dollars and cents. No freighter who wished to remain solvent would carry mail without a government contract.

As he expected, they listened to his proposal in frowning silence.

"It'll cost plenty," objected Majors, who was always the most cautious of the three.

"Thousands of dollars!" Russell agreed blandly.

"Sounds foolish—a *pony* express."

"Ponies will wallop stages—for speed."

Majors snorted, "On a race track!"

"Guess you've got a government contract lined·up," put in Waddell.

"I talked it over with Senator Gwin. We have to show them first."

"We're not pouring our good money into a harebrained scheme," declared Majors.

Russell stiffened. He had a stubborn streak. "See here," he snapped. "I gave my word to Gwin. If you fellows back out, I'll go it alone."

"Get off your high horse, Bill," Waddell said, good-naturedly. "We've done well, sticking together. We'll stick together on this. We'll go along. You agree, Alex?"

Majors nodded reluctantly.

So the Pony Express was born.

3

A Daring Venture

MAIL TO BE RUSHED WEST BY RACING PONIES!
BUTTERFIELD STAGE TIME CUT IN HALF!
TEN DAYS FROM COAST TO COAST!

The news spread fast. It blazed from newspaper headlines. It was discussed around potbellied stoves in frontier stores. It was hailed with joy in isolated mining camps. It stirred half a million settlers in that new empire west of the towering Sierra Nevada mountains.

Everyone assumed that the venture was Government backed. But despite Senator Gwin's fiery oratory, no Government subsidy was provided. Congress was caught in the growing tension between North and South. Deep matters of policy were involved, of which few were aware.

The thorny subject of slavery threatened to split the country. Soon it was to plunge them into bitter conflict. In the event of

PONY EXPRESS!

CHANGE OF

TIME!

REDUCED

RATES!

10 Days to San Francisco!

LETTERS

WILL BE RECEIVED AT THE

OFFICE, 84 BROADWAY,

NEW YORK,

Up to **4** P. M. every TUESDAY,

AND

Up to **2$\frac{1}{2}$** P. M. every SATURDAY,

Which will be forwarded to connect with the PONY EXPRESS leaving
ST. JOSEPH, Missouri,

Every WEDNESDAY and SATURDAY at 11 P. M.

TELEGRAMS

Sent to Fort Kearney on the mornings of MONDAY and FRIDAY, will connect with **PONY** leaving St. Joseph, WEDNESDAYS and SATURDAYS.

EXPRESS CHARGES.

LETTERS weighing half ounce or under.............$1 00
For every additional half ounce or fraction of an ounce 1 00
In all cases to be enclosed in 10 cent Government Stamped Envelopes,

And all Express **CHARGES** Pre-paid.

☞ PONY EXPRESS ENVELOPES For Sale at our Office.

WELLS, FARGO & CO., Ag'ts.

New York, July 1, 1861.

Poster, dated 1861, announces
Pony Express schedule.

war, the gold shipped from California would be badly needed by both sides, but the South hoped to drain gold out of California by means of Butterfield's southern route. For this reason Southern congressmen blocked every effort of Northerners to subsidize a mail route across the northern plains.

William Russell, however, had never been a quitter. He had promised Gwin he'd have the Pony Express operating within sixty-five days. He would!

Over the 1,966-mile route 138 relay stations were required. "Home" stations, where riders were to be posted, would be 75 miles apart. Between them, at 15- to 20-mile intervals, smaller stations would house fresh mounts. Mail would be rushed between St. Joseph and San Francisco in a gigantic relay race. Each rider —each link in the chain—would pass the *mochila* of mail to the next. In order to maintain the utmost speed, a fresh saddle horse would be held ready at each relay station. When a rider raced to the end of his "run" he would pick up mail consigned in the opposite direction and rush back. Thus the *mochilas* of mail would speed east and west, night and day, without pause.

Russell's agents bought only the finest horses. There were two reasons: speed and safety. Riding alone, Express riders couldn't risk fighting Indians, so they would have to outrun them. Their only chance of escape would be to ride horses that were faster and hardier than those of their pursuers. Kentucky thoroughbreds were bought for the flat prairie stretches. Mustangs, carefully selected for toughness and speed, were acquired for the rugged western terrain. The going price for saddle horses was $50, but the Pony Express paid from $150 to $200.

Good horses were useless without good men to ride them. The quality of the riders came above everything. The Express had its pick. Men of all types crowded the divisional offices across the country—tough Mormon farm lads; happy-go-lucky cowboys; weathered stagecoach drivers; seasoned Army scouts. All were eager to carry the mail. The pay was good: $50 a month and up, plus board. But the prestige was even more attractive. Only eighty men were to be hired, and the entire nation would be watching. Many would have ridden just for the glory.

Russell's instructions were simple. He didn't want drinkers and he didn't want reckless adventurers. He was looking for young, rawhide-tough riders of good character who knew the terrain through which they would ride. They had to be physically fit and fearless. Their weight must be under 125 pounds. Twenty was the preferred age, but many who signed up were still in their teens.

Each man was given a small, leatherbound Bible and was required to sign this pledge:

"I do hereby swear before the Great and living God that during my engagement and while I am an employee of Russell, Majors & Waddell, I will, under no circumstances, use profane language; that I will drink no intoxicating liquors; that I will not quarrel or fight with any other employee of the firm, and that in every respect I will conduct myself honestly, be faithful to my duties, and so direct all my acts to win the confidence of my employers.

So help me God."

A Pony Express rider might forget to memorize this rather

lengthy pledge, but he never forgot one unwritten rule:

MAIL FIRST: HORSE SECOND: SELF LAST.

Joe Slade, a rough frontiersman, was hiring riders at Horseshoe Station, Wyoming. A boy jingled in wearing a stained buckskin shirt, shabby jeans and rundown riding boots. A battered old Stetson was jammed on his tangled mop of hair and a gunbelt was buckled around his waist. From the holster protruded the butt of a Colt revolving pistol.

"Wal, boy?" said Slade.

"I want a job, riding mail."

Slade chuckled, "Come back, say, in five years."

"I want that job now."

"Shucks! You ain't a day over fourteen."

"You're a liar! You take that back." The boy grabbed the butt of his Colt, ready to draw on the burly Slade. Out West, to call a man a liar was to invite gunplay.

Something about the boy's manner and the cold challenge in his steady eyes made Slade pause.

"What's your name?" he asked.

"They call me Buffalo Billy."

"You ride?"

"Anything you can cinch a saddle on."

"You're hired!"

William Cody, alias Buffalo Bill, the youngest Pony Express rider, was actually fifteen years old. Slade's hunch paid off. Young Cody could ride anything, anywhere. On one occasion, when his relief failed to show up, he rode 320 miles continuously in 21 hours and 40 minutes to get the mail through. Later, of course, he became famous as Buffalo Bill.

Russell forged ahead with his preparations. The 1,966-mile route was divided into five sections, with a superintendent in charge of each. Ben Ficklin supervised the entire route. Behind them all was the driving energy of William H. Russell.

With the deadline less than two months away, the section bosses faced what seemed to be an impossible task. Stations had to be located, built, and equipped. Riders, station keepers, stock tenders had to be hired. Horses needed to be bought and distributed in groups of two to five among the relay stations. Supplies had to be freighted across hundreds of miles of rough terrain.

A partial list of equipment for one "home" station looked like this:

> FOOD—hams, bacon, flour, pickles, tripe, syrup, salt, tea, coffee, dried fruits, cornmeal.
>
> HOUSEKEEPING—brooms, tin dishes, kettles, plates, mugs, wood and tin buckets, blankets, towels, scissors, needles & thread, stove, hammers, saw, axes, nails.
>
> HORSES—brushes, currycombs, horseshoe nails, manure forks, bridles, horse liniment, rope, farrier's tools.
>
> MEDICINE—turpentine, castor oil, copperas, borax, cream of tartar.
>
> MISC.—wagon grease, tin safe, twine, putty, screws, monkey wrenches, etc., etc.

But first the station had to be built.

The system used by Bolivar Roberts, who handled the stretch between Robert's Creek and Sacramento, was typical. Roberts hired twenty-one men as riders and packers. He bought 129 mules and 100 horses, in addition to bridles, blankets, tools, food, and equipment for the stations. Loading his supplies on wagons, he set out with horses, mules, and men. The train moved slowly along the route as the men built stations and equipped them.

Stations were of many types. Where timber was available they were constructed of logs. On the bare stretches of Nevada and Utah they were made of adobe, or rock. Some were just caves, hollowed in a hillside, with a facing of logs. Each had a corral, and shelter stalls for the ponies.

A station keeper was in charge, with a stock tender to assist. At the "home" stations, where riders ate and slept, there were two to five stock tenders. These men were to lead a lonely dangerous life. They proved to be sitting ducks for roaming bands of Indians. Later, many an Express rider was to dash up to an isolated station and find the occupants butchered, the stock stolen, and the place gutted.

The men and horses of the Pony Express were carefully selected, and so was their equipment. The Express saddle was light and specially designed. Covering it was something new, something the riders would learn to treasure above their own lives—the *mochila*. *Mochila* and saddle together weighed less than the standard stock saddle. The total weight a pony was allowed to carry was 165 pounds, including the rider and twenty pounds of mail.

Express riders were issued bright red shirts and blue pants. Many, however, preferred to wear range garb—a flannel shirt, sleeveless vest, and denim pants tucked into the uppers of riding boots. A Stetson, beloved of every western rider, covered the head, and a gunbelt circled the waist. In addition to a Colt revolver, they were issued bowie knives and lightweight rifles. Many discarded the rifles to save weight. They were also given horns, in order to

signal their approach to relay stations so that remounts might be ready. Few ever used them.

The days were speeding by, and the third of April, 1860, when Russell had promised to launch the service, drew close.

At scores of stations—on the plains of Kansas, the deserts of Utah, the sage flats of Nevada; amid the rugged hills of Wyoming, the breaks of Nebraska; the slopes of the Sierra Nevadas—riders and stock tenders were poised, waiting.

But the enormous task of building stations clear across the United States, equipping them, buying horses, and hiring men, was still unfinished. The starting date couldn't be postponed. It had been advertised in newspapers throughout the country and mail was already piling up. The rate for letters was $3 for each half-ounce if carried from either end of the line to Salt Lake City, which lay roughly midway. To all points beyond it was $5. Letters

The Pony Express station at Gothenburg, Nebraska.

were written on tissue paper to reduce weight and each envelope carried a ten-cent U.S. postage stamp. The letters were also wrapped in oiled silk to keep them dry when Express riders forded streams. With full *cantinas* a pony could carry a pay load of $3,200.

Every rider knew his schedule by heart. For example, five days less four hours was allowed from San Francisco to Salt Lake City. Less than five days to cover close to a thousand miles! This was better time than ever before! There was no allowance for delay or error. No margin was allowed for unknown obstacles—swollen rivers, blocked mountain passes, ravaging Indians. Every rider along that 1,966-mile chain *had* to be on time, not just once, but this week, next week, every week. Otherwise Russell's claim that he could furnish reliable mail service across America in ten days became an empty boast—and his hope of earning a government subsidy a dream.

Many doubted the riders could keep any kind of a schedule. Wagers were freely made that the "whole crazy project" would collapse in a month. Newspapers debated the question endlessly. It was generally agreed that no one could run a pony express over arid deserts, across Indian territory, and through rugged mountain country, on a schedule, like an eastern railway train. Wasn't the best time a rider had ever made across the plains—using relays of horses—seventeen days and twelve hours?

The Pony Express proposed to cut this in half, and to continue cutting it in half, month after month.

"It can't be done!" declared the doubters. Meanwhile the entire nation watched and waited.

A Pony Express postage stamp.

4

Those Who Tried —And Failed

The doubters could point to a decade of failure. Ever since the discovery of gold in California the Post Office had striven to speed up mail service to and from the Pacific Coast. Between East and West, however, lay the "Great American Desert." This vast, unexplored region stretched from the Missouri River in the east to the Sierra Nevada Mountains in the west, close to 2,000 miles. Immigrant trains took four to six months to cross it. Their trails were marked by broken-down wagons, discarded goods, the bleached bones of oxen, and many lonely graves.

"It is plain," declared the postmaster-general, "that a fast overland route is out of the question." So he had turned to the sea.

In 1848, a contract was made with the Pacific Mail Steamship

Company to carry mail from New York to the Pacific Coast. For this the steamship company was to receive a $199,000 annual subsidy. Three steamships, the *California,* the *Panama,* and the *Oregon,* were built to carry the mail. Postage was set at 40¢ a letter.

After the fiasco of the *California,* which was deserted by her crew when she docked in San Francisco, the *Oregon* arrived in San Francisco Bay. Her captain took the precaution of dropping anchor under the guns of a man o' war in order to keep his rebellious crew on board. They threatened mutiny. The sailors were finally pacified when their wages were raised from $12 to $112 per month. On April 12, 1849, the *Oregon* steamed away with the first consignment of mail for the East.

From then on, despite desertions and other difficulties, the Pacific Mail Steamship Company maintained a more or less regular service between New York and San Francisco. By packing the mail across the Isthmus of Panama by muleback, twenty-two-day mail service was provided.

Californians, however, were still dissatisfied. "Why does our mail have to be carried halfway around the world?" they demanded. "Why do we have to wait two months or more for a reply to a letter sent east?"

The Mormons, whose capital, Salt Lake City, was located roughly halfway across the plains, had even greater cause for complaint. They were, they said, completely without mail service and cut off from the rest of the world.

So, in 1850, the harried Post Office Department had made a contract with Samuel H. Woodson to carry mail from the Missouri River to Salt Lake City. For providing monthly service, Woodson was to receive $19,500 a year. He began service on July 1, 1850, packing the mail on muleback. The time allowed for a trip was thirty days.

Through that summer, despite Indian raids, Woodson delivered the mail. When winter came, and biting blizzards swept the plains, it was a different story. True, Woodson and his muleteers made heroic efforts to get the mail through. On the November trip, carrying mail to Salt Lake City, their weary animals bogged down in deep snowdrifts. The men dragged the mail sacks over the frozen ground for forty miles, crossing the Wasatch Mountains. Half-dead from exposure and exhaustion, they finally staggered into Salt Lake City.

When they left Salt Lake with the December mail, Woodson and his men found the trails impassable and were compelled to turn back.

In December, 1853, Governor Brigham Young, of Utah, mourned, "We have been without a solitary mail for over half a year at a time."

Next, four-horse coaches were tried, with a schedule of thirty days between Independence, Missouri, and Salt Lake City. Indians constantly harassed the line, and drivers frequently had to dump their load of mail to make a getaway. It is said that letters from plundered stages were scattered like snow over the prairie. On May 2, 1860, the *Deserat News* reported, "An ox-wagon load of mail bags that had been left by the wayside, some of them for six months, arrived Wednesday night, the 25th . . . comprising dates from November, 1859 to April, 1860." The line was finally forced out of business.

A tough Mormon, Hiram Kimball, tackled the job, using wagons. He only succeeded in getting one mail through during an entire winter.

Carrying mail across the "Great American Desert," was a heart-breaking, back-breaking business.

Meanwhile, in California, Absalom Woodward and Major George Chorpenning, both hardy frontiersmen, obtained a contract from the Government to carry mail between Placerville, California, and Salt Lake City. The 910-mile trail across Nevada and western Utah passed over what was probably the most desolate terrain in the West. For monthly service, they were to receive $19,000 annually.

On May 1, 1851, the bearded miners of Hangtown gave the first consignment of mail an hilarious send-off for Salt Lake City. (Placerville was then known as Hangtown, due to the many malefactors who, as citizens expressed it, were "hung up to dry.") This was an epoch-making event—the first mail service direct to the East. Major Chorpenning, an experienced Indian fighter, was in charge of the string of mules upon which the mail sacks were carried. With him were several armed men.

The last diamond hitch was tightened and the nodding mules plodded out of town. Beyond the long and rocky trail that snaked across the Sierras, through Carson Pass, lay vast plains clothed with dusty gray-green sage, and spotted with gleaming white alkali sinks. For hundreds of miles not a single white man's habitation was to be found. The waste was peopled only by bands of marauding Paiutes.

Despite brushes with Indians, the train got through, as did

Absalom Woodward's train, crisscrossing from the opposite direction, with mail from Salt Lake City.

But winter brought trouble. Woodward left Sacramento City in November with the usual mule train, guarded by four armed men. Storms and snow-choked trails in the Sierras held them up. They finally broke through and reached the open plains beyond, now a gleaming expanse of snow. As the string of men and mules pushed across the snow, hovering Paiutes continually threatened to attack. Camping overnight at Stockton Springs, 150 miles from Salt Lake City, they met the westbound train, under Major Chorpenning. Woodward cautioned Chorpenning against Indians and the two trains parted.

Woodward and his party were never seen again alive.

Chorpenning and his men fought their way westward, beating off Paiute attacks day after day. One man was wounded, five horses were killed, but they got through.

In December and again in January, the mail trains were unable to cross the snowbound Sierra Nevada Mountains. Desperate to save his mail contract—which called for monthly service—Chorpenning directed Edson Cody, in charge of the February mail train to Salt Lake City, to circle northward through the Feather River country.

Battling storm and blizzard, Cody and his men took forty days to reach Carson Valley, Nevada. Here they obtained fresh animals and pushed on toward Salt Lake City. It was bitter cold. One night, in the Goose Creek Mountains, every animal—thirteen mules and one horse—froze to death. Living on frozen flesh hacked off the dead mules, Cody and his men struggled on with the mail sacks on their backs. Afoot, they toiled across two hundred miles of frozen terrain. For the first seven days they lived on the mule meat; for the four remaining days, still struggling through the snow, they starved. But they delivered the mail at Salt Lake City!

March found Major Chorpenning in Salt Lake City with a load of westbound mail and no helpers. In vain he tried to enlist men by offering premium pay. But after the mysterious disappearance of the Woodward party and the privations suffered by Edson Cody and his men, no one was willing to venture across the icy Paiute-infested waste for any kind of money.

Chorpenning decided to take the mail through alone. Leading a string of laden mules, he headed out into the frozen wilderness. Incredibly, he got the mail through to California. How, no one will ever know. Chorpenning was a close-mouthed man and he never discussed the trip. It was believed that he was able to evade hostile Indians by hiding during the day and travelling at night.

With the spring thaw, the fate of Woodward and his party was revealed. The hacked remains of four men were found in the Big Canyon of the Humboldt River. From an Indian it was learned that they had been attacked, and fought until their ammunition was exhausted, and died. The mules had been stolen and the mail destroyed. Woodward, although wounded, had broken through the cordon of Paiutes and had ridden 150 miles across country before another party of hostile Indians cut him down.

Back in Washington, D.C., the Government failed to appreciate Major Chorpenning's superhuman efforts to live up to his contract —it was cancelled on the grounds of "inadequate service."

Men of Chorpenning's breed never admit defeat. In April, 1854, he obtained a second contract. This time he used a more southerly route, through San Bernardino to San Diego. By so doing he avoided the snow-blocked Sierra passes. But Indians couldn't be avoided; they buzzed around his mail trains like hornets. Again and again, they murdered his men, destroyed the mail, looted his pack mules. It proved impossible to maintain regular service. Again his mail contract was cancelled.

By now mail was proceeding steadily to and from the East, via the steamships of Pacific Mail. The sea route was long and tedious, but the mail *WAS* delivered. There were no Indians to waylay and destroy it.

Californians still stubbornly insisted that the quickest, most logical route between East and West was across the "Great American Desert." Finally, in 1858, they succeeded in bringing the postmaster general around to their point of view. There was general rejoicing when he announced that the Government would subsidize a new weekly mail route, between Hangtown, California and Salt Lake City, Utah. And the man with whom the contract was signed was the indefatigable Major Chorpenning!

This new service was on a much larger scale than either of the Major's two previous efforts. He was to receive a subsidy of $190,000 a year, and would use Concord stage coaches. Chorpenning was determined to succeed on his third attempt. It is said that he spent over $300,000 building stations and buying equipment. Teams would be changed every twenty to forty miles at stations along the route.

The mail went through. Occasionally it was delayed by an Indian attack or by snow-blocked passes. Again the Government complained of "inadequate service." At the end of the year Chorpenning received only $130,000, $60,000 less than the contract called for. Then his subsidy was reduced to $80,000 a year. Losing money on every trip, he strove to make good—in vain. In May, 1860, his contract was cancelled for "repeated failures."

Major Chorpenning's reward for nine years of dauntless endeavor was bankruptcy.

Camels came next. Jefferson Davis, Secretary of War, suggested they be tried. "What animal is better fitted to cross the Great American Desert than the camel?" he demanded. "Is not its natural habitat the sandy desert of the Sahara? Would it not be at home on the vast barren plains of America?"

Magazine writers and newspaper editors were enthusiastic. Wasn't the camel fleeter than the horse, stronger than the mule, tougher than the ox? Wouldn't the "ship of the desert" solve the difficult problem of conveying mail between East and West?

Congress passed a bill to launch the camel project in 1855. Seventy-five camels were purchased in Arabia, and in due time they arrived in America. As an experiment, Lieutenant Edward F. Beale was directed to use them for transportation during the survey of a road from Fort Defiance, Arizona, to the Grand Canyon.

It quickly became apparent that American livestock—horses, mules, oxen—disliked camels. There was no surer way to stir every pony dozing at the hitchrails of a western cowtown into snorting, hoof-lashing frenzy than to lead just one camel down Main Street. One whiff of a camel threw placid ox teams that were hauling freight wagon into terror-stricken confusion.

Those camels stirred up more trouble in Arizona than a dozen Apache war parties.

Another difficulty arose. Camels, which were accustomed to soft, yielding sand, quickly became lame on the rocky trails of the West. The ingenious Lieutenant Beale devised leather boots, but the camels quickly made it plain that they preferred their feet bare. All in all, the sorely-tried Beale, whose gawky charges were regarded with hostility by every cowpuncher, bullwhacker, and muleskinner on the trail, had a hard time.

In addition, the ungainly brutes did not prove to be more speedy than horses; they could not carry greater burdens farther than mules, and they were certainly not tougher than oxen.

It became apparent that the American West was no place for them, and the project was allowed to die a quiet death. Some of the animals went to circuses. Many broke away—or were released —and disappeared into the desert. For years afterward travelers camping at isolated waterholes were apt to be scared out of their wits when the huge, ungainly form of a lonely camel padded silently out of the night.

So the problem of fast mail service to the West was still unsolved. It seemed that the "Great American Desert" with its two thousand-mile span of arid plains, rugged mountains, and hostile Indians presented an impassable barrier—until William H. Russell conceived the idea of a pony express.

All else had failed—mules, wagons, stages, and camels. Would the Pony Express prove to be another fiasco?

Tuesday, April 3, 1860, dawned. This day would tell.

5

The First Ride

At five p.m., April 3, Bill Richardson, itching to ride, led his bay mare back and forth in front of the Pattee House, St. Joseph. He had been selected to carry the mail over the first lap of the westward race. Richardson was dark and wiry, and he made a striking picture in his red shirt, blue pants, fringed buckskin jacket and fancy high boots, the "official" costume of the Pony Express riders. Again and again he glanced at the face of his silver-cased watch. The mail was scheduled to leave at five o'clock. The hands of the watch crept around to 5:30, 5:45, 6:00—and still no mail!

An hilarious crowd surged around the Express Rider. Everyone had come to town to see the Pony Express launched, even those who doubted that the mail would ever reach San Francisco. The Pattee House, claimed by many to be the finest hostelry on the river, was crowded with guests. Flags were flying and bunting was draped on the wooden canopies of stores. A brass band played martial music. The militia was on parade. This day would put St. Joseph on the map. Already it was a stagecoach terminus and was linked by railway with Hannibal. The whole nation knew that it had been selected as the jumping off point for the Pony Express. St. Joseph sure had a rosy future, folks said. Maybe it would become as important as Chicago! Well, maybe St. Louis.

It was well past six o'clock now. The sun sank in a blaze of scarlet. The crowd, restless and bored with waiting, had begun to press around Richardson, plucking hairs from his pony's mane and tail to weave into rings and watch chains as souvenirs. In no good humor, Richardson led his pony back to the stable.

But Major Jeff Thompson, William Russell and Alexander Majors, waiting in the Pattee House, weren't too concerned. A message had come through by telegraph stating that the train carrying the mail to St. Joseph would be several hours late.

Supt. J. T. K. Haywood of the Hannibal & St. Joseph Railroad was not to blame. He was just as anxious as Bill Richardson to rush the mail through. He had his eye on a mail contract, too! All this time mail had been brought to St. Joseph by river steamer. Here was a splendid opportunity to show how much more reliably the railroad could handle it—and how much faster.

For hours, the best locomotive on the line, the "Missouri," had been hissing under steam at Hannibal. A specially-built mail car, with several built-in seats for railway officials, was hitched onto its tender. At the throttle was Addison Clerk, reputedly the best engineer on the road. The line had been cleared of all other rolling stock to give Clerk a clear run through.

The delay was caused by the special messenger carrying mail from Washington, D. C. He had stopped off at New York to pick up copies of *The New York Herald and Tribune,* which had been specially printed on tissue paper, and he had somehow missed a railway connection. When he finally arrived at Hannibal he was two-and-a-half hours late. He had barely stepped aboard when Clerk opened up the throttle—and held it open all the way!

In those days freight trains had a top speed of 15 miles per hour; passenger trains were limited to 24 miles per hour. Higher speeds were dangerous on the lightly built roadbeds.

For the first fifty miles out of Hannibal the track was level and straight. Men swore that Clerk tore over it at 60 miles per hour. Ashen-faced, the august railway officials clung grimly to their seats as the car rocked to and fro. They never forgot that ride.

At Macon, the engine, a wood burner, had to be re-fueled. L. S. Coleman, the fuel agent, had built a rough platform beside the track, tender-high. Men crowded on this platform, elbow to elbow. Each clutched as much dry cottonwood as he could hold to his chest. As the engine slowed down, every man dumped his armful of wood into the tender. Coleman stood timing them with his watch. The train stopped exactly fifteen seconds. Clerk eased back the throttle again and the "special" roared away.

Beyond Macon a steep grade ran down to the Carlton River; then the line twisted through rough country, with numerous grades and curves. Fire streaming from the big smokestack, sparks showering, the "Missouri" hurtled along the tracks.

The distant screech of an engine whistle told the crowds at St. Joseph that their wait was nearing an end. When the "special" rolled into the depot, Engineer Clerk, shirt grimy, features sooted, stepped onto the platform with a triumphant smile. His passengers sighed with relief!

Time for the 206-mile run was 4 hours and 51 minutes. Clerk had made a record run that would not be equalled for another fifty years.

Richardson had already brought his bay back to the front of the Pattee House. The *mochila* lay across the saddle, its *cantinas* holding a copy of the *St. Joseph Gazette,* and local letters. The newly arrived mail was added, but Richardson, although he was already late, could not leave yet. There were speeches to be made! Mayor Thompson spoke glowingly of the future; Alexander Majors prophesied that steel would eventually span the continent. Bill Russell, the driving force behind it all, said nothing.

A cannon boomed. Richardson swung into the saddle. At 7:15 p.m. he headed for the ferry that would carry him across the river to Edward, Kansas, where his long ride would begin. On the boat he changed his red shirt and blue pants for more workmanlike gray flannel shirt and jeans. When he left the ferry he set out to make time. Already the mail was two hours and fifteen minutes late. The bay thundered along the trail. Ahead, strung across the continent, was a chain 1,966 miles long with eager riders waiting for their turn to rush the *mochila* through to San Francisco.

Three times Richardson switched mounts—at Troy, Kennekuk, and Kickapoo. At 11:30 p.m. he tore into Granada, the end of his run. He'd cut forty-five minutes off the lost time.

Don Rising, the next rider, had been fretting for hours. Two minutes were allowed for the transfer of the *mochila.* Rising flung it across his mount in seconds, leaped upon his pony and thundered away. Dawn found him at Marysville, the end of his run, with Jack Keetley ready to rush the mail on to Big Sandy.

So the *mochila* sped on, from rider to rider. At dawn on April 9, it reached Salt Lake City, halfway across the continent. Now it was 18 hours and 45 minutes behind schedule! Although the Pony Express riders had spared neither themselves nor their mounts, storms, swollen streams, and boggy trails had slowed them down.

At Julesburg the eastbound rider almost lost both his life and the mail in the Platte River. The stream was a raging yellow flood, swollen bank-high by heavy rains. The Express rider had plunged in and had tried to swim his pony across. The pony was swept downstream. Horse and rider rolled over and over, tossed in the swirling current. Half-drowned, the rider clung to his *mochila* and managed to struggle ashore. Streaming water, he acquired another pony and dashed on.

In San Francisco, the launching of the Pony Express created a little less excitement than it had at St. Joseph. The *Alta California* had announced that the first rider, James Randall, would leave at 4 p.m., on April 3, from the Alta Telegraph Office, on Montgomery Street. A crowd gathered to watch the event. Randall's mount, "a nankeen colored pony," was decorated with miniature flags. The *mochila,* whose *cantinas* contained 85 letters, was set across the saddle and Randall attempted to mount—from the wrong side! The pony objected. There was some confusion. Randall corrected his mistake and the crowd cheered. The rider headed for the waterfront, where the stern-wheeler *Antelope* was waiting. Here he handed over the *mochila* to the purser. The *Antelope* took off, while Randall quietly returned his mount to its stable. Both he and his pony had been part of a show. The *real* rider, Billy Hamilton, was to pick up the *mochila* at Sacramento.

It was pitch black, a heavy rain was falling, the water streamed off the piles of merchandise dumped on the dock when the *Antelope* tied up at Sacramento, ten hours later, at 2 a.m. Not a human being was in sight, with the exception of Hamilton, who stood beside his dripping mount, and the local Express agent.

The agent hurried up the gangplank, took over the *mochila,* quickly inserted mail collected at Sacramento in a *cantina* and locked it. Then he handed the *mochila* to Hamilton and Billy was off, heading toward the Sierras.

The trail was sodden. Rain drummed down. It was, to quote Billy, "as black as the inside of a cow," and he had 57 miles to ride. Fresh saddle horses were waiting at Five Mile House, Fifteen Mile House, Mormon Tavern, and Hangtown. At each station he was out of one saddle and into the other in seconds, determined not to fall behind schedule. When he reached the end of his run, Sportsman's Hall, he had trimmed 30 minutes from his allotted time.

Warren Upson, son of the editor of *The Sacramento Union,* was the next rider. Upson faced what was probably the toughest ride along the 1,966-mile route. The narrow, twisting trail snaked upward, ever upward, winding up the flanks of the mighty Sierra Nevadas. Driving rain turned into sleet, and snow began to pile up, slowing the pony to a walk.

Stages of the Carson City Line, which regularly crossed the mountains, had been halted, snowed in at Strawberry Valley. The vast barn at Sportsman's Hall was packed with the teams of freighters who had found the trail impassable. Many a bet was made that young Upson would never cross the mountains. But the young Express rider stubbornly pushed on, struggling up toward the snow-covered peaks. Icy winds howled through the funnel of the pass and powdery snow swirled into his face, almost blinding him. Again and again, he was forced to dismount and lead his pony. He never realized that he had crossed the summit of the pass until he felt the trail heading downward. True, the snow was still deep and the blizzard froze the very marrow of his bones, but the going was easier.

He changed horses at Strawberry, Hope Valley, Woodbridge, and Genoa, all of which were snowed in. Toward midnight he rode into Carson City, the end of his run, exhausted, with 85 arduous miles behind him.

Between Carson City and Salt Lake City lay a six-hundred-mile expanse of snow-covered plains, grained by hummocky ridges. Forty-seven lonely relay stations, 12 to 15 miles apart, were dotted across this spread of frozen terrain.

From station to station the mail sped, passed from rider to rider, each racing at breakneck speed. When the *mochila* arrived at the Pony Express office on State Street, Salt Lake City, 103 hours and 45 minutes had elapsed since it left Sacramento. The scheduled time was 110 hours.

East- and west-bound riders hurtled past each other somewhere east of Salt Lake.

At five p.m., April 13, Bill Richardson rode off the river ferry, pushed through cheering crowds and dismounted outside the Pattee House, St. Joseph. The mail was on schedule!

That night St. Joseph staged a celebration that put the Fourth of July to shame. Bonfires blazed, fireworks soared against the starlit sky, church bells pealed, and the cannon that had signalled the start ten days before boomed again.

The west-bound *mochila* reached Warren Upson at Carson City on April 12, at 3:30 p.m.—on schedule, despite time lost due to the late start, flooding rivers, and soggy trails. Upson hit back for the Sierras, a great white-crested wall blocking out the western horizon. Word of his departure was flashed by telegraph to Sacramento and San Francisco. Snow had stopped falling in the mountains, but Upson bucked another obstacle. The narrow, rock-girt trail was blocked by an endless procession of freight wagons and mule trains, carrying supplies to the Carson Valley mines. Held up by the storm, they now flowed into Nevada.

The Express rider was forced to leave the regular trail and flounder through snow drifts. One hour after noon, he reached Sportsman's Hall, and passed the *mochila* to Bill Hamilton for the last run to Sacramento.

On his outward trip, Hamilton had ridden in solitude, unnoticed in rain-sodden darkness. Now, to his amazement, cheering crowds greeted him in Hangtown—but that was nothing compared to the royal welcome that awaited him in Sacramento.

Almost a hundred horsemen were waiting at Sutter's Fort to escort him into town. Flags decorated public buildings and were draped over awnings. When the dust of his escort boiled on the Fort Sutter road, fire engine bells clanged, church bells rang, guns boomed. A cannon, planted in the square, greeted him with a succession of forty roaring blasts. Amid the uproar—the din of the cannon, the jangling bells, the brass bands—the astounded Hamilton rode into Sacramento, while citizens swarming on roof tops yelled greetings and women threw flowers and kisses.

The celebration in San Francisco.

Eventually, the Express rider made his way through the mob of cheering citizens to the dock, where the *Antelope* had delayed its departure an hour to await him. This time he carried the *mochila* through to San Francisco.

Even the stern-wheeler made a record run down to the Bay city. It tied up amid the clamor of ringing bells and the flare of bursting rockets. Bonfires flamed at street corners. When Hamilton rode his pony off the boat it was close to midnight, but a parade formed and triumphantly led him through streets that were thick with cheering crowds. Ahead of him blaring "See the Conquering Hero Comes," marched the California band, followed by Hook and Ladder Company #2, Engine Companies #5 and #6. Behind him streamed a motley of men afoot and on horseback, all yelling themselves hoarse. One woman darted off the plankwalk, snatched off her fancy bonnet and clapped it over the Express pony's ears.

The parade halted at the Alta Express Company's office and Hamilton handed over the battered *mochila* that had travelled 1,966 miles from St. Joseph, Missouri. And battered it was! One hundred thirty-eight ponies had raced that stout sheet of leather with its four locked *cantinas* through snow and storm, over deserts, across mountains, through streams. And they'd rushed it across the continent on schedule. It had left St. Joseph at 7:15 p.m., April 3, and arrived at Sacramento at 5:30 p.m. April 13. It contained, besides the tissue-printed newspapers, 49 letters and five telegrams, including one telegram of congratulations from President Buchanan.

William Russell and his daredevil riders had made good.

But the critics said, "A publicity stunt. Bill Russell can't keep it up."

6

Disaster

For one full month William Russell's hardy Pony Express riders proved they could indeed "keep it up." Without a break, they made good on their proud slogan "Ten Days from Coast to Coast."

Then disaster struck.

On the morning of May 8, 1860, Tom Flynn approached Williams station at full gallop. Flynn was rushing the *mochila* eastward. As he drew closer to the lonely station on the big bend of the Carson River, he sensed that something was wrong. Usually, his remount stood, ready rigged, outside the station, its bridle held by Jim Fleming or Dutch Phil, ready for the *mochila* to be slung across its saddle. Today there was no horse, no sign of life. Black buzzards—harbingers of death—slowly circled overhead.

A cold chill ran down Flynn's spine when he reined up and dismounted. Two bodies were sprawled on the sandy ground by the station doorway. The feathered shafts of arrows protruded from the limp forms. One glance and the horrified Flynn knew they were David and Oscar Williams, brothers of the station keeper.

Sickened, he peered across the threshold. The bloody remains of Jim Fleming and Dutch Phil were stretched on the packed earth floor, amid spilled flour, beans, and smashed kitchen utensils.

Flynn didn't have to guess who had murdered the crew and sacked the station. "Paiutes!" he muttered, whirled around and rushed for his pony. Maybe the savages were concealed in the sagebrush, waiting to trap him. A flying leap and he straddled his mount. Frantically, he spurred for the nearest settlement, Virginia City.

Long before a white man ever ventured into the vast spread of country that lay between Salt Lake and the Sierras, the Paiutes (or Pah-Utes) had roamed its barren plains and lurked in its desolate mountains. From the first they fought the invasion of the "pale-faces." Although attacks on trappers were recorded as early as 1832, they had never declared war. Their hostilities had been mostly confined to small, sneak attacks—stealing horses, cutting off solitary prospectors, killing isolated settlers.

The discovery of gold on the Comstock Lode several years before had brought a stampede of California prospectors across the Sierras. They had settled by the thousands in and around Alder Gulch, through which the fabulous Comstock vein of gold and silver ran. Shack towns sprang up, of which Virginia City was the wildest. Its dance halls, gambling joints, and saloons never closed.

This picture of the Pony Express rider pursued by Indians first appeared in an English newspaper.

When the Express rider pounded into the unlovely blotch of canvas shelters and rude shacks that was Virginia City, he found the entire camp pulsating with excitement. Ravaging Paiutes had killed eight prospectors, attacked settlers at Honey Lake, driven off cattle, and burned ranches. In a panic, settlers and prospectors from all over were streaming into town, seeking shelter.

The Paiutes were on the warpath. And there were 8,000 of them!

Later, it was learned that Chief Winnemucca had called the tribe together at Pyramid Lake. For months the Paiutes had been restive, angered by the swarms of prospectors that spread over their country. The invaders gophered into the hills, destroyed what little timber there was, ignored the Indians in their eager search for "color."

The winter had been unusually severe. The "palefaces" had cut down most of the piñon trees to feed their camp fires. But the piñon nut provided much of the tribe's food, and many Paiute families were starving. The younger warriors clamored for war. Winnemucca, their old chief, tried to restrain them—in vain.

Flynn found that a volunteer force to subdue the Paiutes was being hastily organized. Like most westerners, the miners had a contempt for the fighting methods of Indians, which were usually to slash and run. A force of a hundred mounted men was considered to be sufficient.

Although a Major William O. Ormsby was named commander, actually he had no authority over these volunteers, who were undrilled and poorly disciplined. Strung over the prairie in a ragged cavalcade, they headed for Williams station, where they buried the four murdered men. They received word that the Indians were gathered in force at Pyramid Lake.

Following a trail along the top of a gorge through which the Truckee River flowed, the volunteers headed for Pyramid Lake. As it approached the lake, the gorge flattened and the trail slanted down to a narrow bench, thickly covered with sagebrush. Beyond the bench stood a grove of cottonwood trees. When Indians were sighted in the cottonwoods, the entire body of volunteers charged for the grove in a disorderly array, the better riders pulling ahead. The yelling mob galloped madly across the sagebrush bench, threaded through the cottonwoods, emerged on the far side—and were greeted by an unexpected shower of arrows. Thrown into confusion, they wheeled and spurred back to the shelter of the cottonwoods.

Hundreds of Indians—previously hidden—rose out of the sage-brush, cutting off further retreat. Milling around in the grove, the bewildered volunteers were attacked on all sides. Too late, Ormsby realized that they had ridden into a trap.

A hail of arrows drove the men out of the cottonwoods. A tangle of riders, mounted on panicky ponies, surged across the bench which immediately became an inferno of squalling ponies, yelling Paiutes, droning arrows, roaring guns. Surrounded, hope-lessly outnumbered, fighting blindly, the volunteers were ruthlessly cut down. The Indians hurled themselves into the melee of horsemen, dragged men from their saddles, knifed them, and hamstrung the ponies. Major Ormsby, striving desperately to straighten out the confusion, was shot in the mouth by a poisoned arrow, then wounded in both arms. He extended his revolver to the Indians raging around, in a gesture of surrender. They promptly killed him.

A number of volunteers finally broke out of the trap and stampeded up the hill to the trail atop the gorge. As they rode, mounted Paiutes knifed through their ranks, dragged them from their ponies and killed them. Less than fifty volunteers survived.

News of the defeat spread panic through the Carson Valley. In Virginia City, a stone house was hastily fortified and the women and children were placed inside. At Carson City, the Penrod Hotel was converted into a fort. At Silver City, a rock redoubt was quickly built on a nearby hill. At any moment the Paiutes were expected to sweep through the cities. Urgent appeals for help sped over the telegraph to California.

The "Golden State" quickly responded. Within two days a force of 165 men was organized at Downieville. They marched to Virginia City afoot, and reached it in five days. Other settlements like Sacramento, Placerville, Nevada City sent volunteers. The Army dispatched 150 men of the 3rd Infantry. By the end of May 800 men were under arms, of which 200 were regular United States soldiers.

On May 26, this force, under the command of Colonel Hayes, headed for Pyramid Lake. It was at this time that Bob Haslam made his historic ride, recounted earlier. At this time, too, another Express rider—whose name has been lost—rode into Dry Creek station, sagging in the saddle. An arrow was sunk deep in his back, and blood soaked the *mochila*. Before he could be carried into the station, he died.

At Williams station, a large band of Paiutes, now convinced that the "palefaces" could be defeated, attacked Colonel Hayes' force. After a brisk skirmish, in which two volunteers and six Indians were killed, the Paiutes retreated. They withdrew toward Pyramid Lake.

Colonel Hayes' scouts pressed them hard. Reaching their old battleground, where the bodies of volunteers killed in the tragic battle of Pyramid Lake still stiffened, Chief Winnemucca and his braves stood at bay.

For three hours Colonel Hayes' force doggedly pushed the assault. Then the Paiutes broke and retreated. In the pursuit twenty-five Indians were killed and over fifty horses were captured. At dawn it was discovered that the Paiutes had scattered, vanishing into the hills. The Colonel sent out patrols, but the Indians, who were familiar with every foot of the rugged terrain, eluded them. Colonel Hayes marched his force back to Carson City. The Washoe Paiute War was officially over. Actually, the Paiutes, broken up into numerous bands, continued to pillage and kill for many months.

What of the Pony Express? The long chain of stations across Nevada and western Utah were wide open to attack. Relay stations were occupied by only two men, "home" stations seldom by more than five. Spaced 15 to 20 miles apart over six hundred miles of wild terrain, these stations were obviously prey for the raiding Paiutes. Station keepers and stock tenders had no choice but to "fort up" and sell their lives dearly.

Up and down the line, stations were sacked, stock tenders murdered, and ponies were stolen. For three weeks mail accumulated at San Francisco and Salt Lake City. No Express rider, however daring, could cross Paiute country. A score of grim stories flowed out of that ill-fated chain of stations. At least one had a touch of humor.

Elijah J. Wilson, Express rider, and Mike Holt, station keeper, were eating breakfast at Egan's station. Hooves clattered outside. Wilson ran to the doorway—and saw a party of thirty scowling Paiutes.

Yelling to Holt, he slammed the door shut, and dropped the bar securing it into place. Both men grabbed their guns and opened fire through the windows. The yelling Indians raced their ponies around the cabin. Wilson and Holt fired at them until their ammunition ran out. Then the Paiutes broke down the door and flooded in. The two defenders, knives in hand, were backed against the rear wall, determined to fight to the death. A chief held his men back. "Bread!" he grunted.

Hastily, Holt and Wilson piled all the bread they had on the table. The braves seemed to be starving. They snatched up the loaves and tore them to pieces with their fingers. In seconds, every loaf had been consumed.

Several sacks of flour were stacked in a corner. By pointing and gesturing, the chief made it clear that he wanted the white men to bake more bread.

The two men got busy. All through the day they labored, white with flour, mixing dough and baking bread. Each hot loaf was eagerly grabbed by the impatient Indians clustered around them.

Toward sundown the last sack of flour ran out. Before the two unfortunate bakers could resist, they were seized, and hustled outside, their arms bound behind them. While two Paiutes busied themselves sinking the end of a wagon tongue into the ground to serve as a stake, others gathered sagebrush. The Indians lashed Wilson and Holt to opposite sides of the stake and piled brush around them. A Paiute set light to the brush and the Indians gathered in a circle.

At this point, another Express rider, William Dennis, approached with the *mochila*. At sight of the blazing brush, the haggard victims and circling Paiutes, Dennis whirled his pony and dashed away. A mile or so back along the trail he had passed a detachment of United States Dragoons. He raced back to them and told of the tragedy ahead. The Dragoons swept to the rescue. Pounding up to the station, pistols spitting hot lead, they charged the surprised Paiutes. The Indians scattered like a flock of startled quail, and left eighteen dead lying on the ground.

Holt and Wilson were a little scorched—no more!

7

The "Pony" Kicks Back

For one month the "Pony" had galloped to glory. Then, suddenly, not a *mochila* moved. Service was paralyzed.

"See!" mocked the critics. "One Indian outbreak and the Pony Express is finished!"

William W. Finney, Superintendent of the route west of the Sierra Nevadas, had different ideas. Finney was not the type to quit when trouble erupted.

He sought out General Clarke. "Lend me seventy-five soldiers," he begged. "With a military escort I can rebuild the stations across Nevada and get the mail rolling."

But the General declined. He had already sent 150 men to help Colonel Hayes at Carson City. He had only a small force left. Hayes might need more men.

Undaunted, Finney set out for Nevada. Here he found that matters were even worse than he had suspected. Colonel Hayes had not yet led his 800 men against the Paiutes, and the Indians were devastating the entire Territory.

Finney was cut off from headquarters in the East. He had little money. He telegraphed the citizens of Sacramento:

> "Will Sacramento help the Pony in its difficulty? We have conferred some benefits, but asked little, and perhaps the people will assist. Can anything be done in your city towards paying expenses to furnish arms and ammunition for twenty-five men to go through with me to Salt Lake to take and bring on the Express? . . . what is wanted is $1,000 for pay of the men, $500 for provisions, twenty-five Sharp's rifles, and as many dragoon pistols. I will guarantee to keep the Pony alive a little longer."

The response was prompt. In a few days he received the money and arms he needed. But in the midst of organizing a party of Pony Express riders, stock tenders and station keepers, he fell sick. Bolivar Roberts, Superintendent of the division that lay between the California line and Robert's Creek, Nevada, took over. He left Carson City on June 9, with twenty men, and a three-week accumulation of eastbound mail.

Roberts and his men pushed steadily ahead, rebuilding each wrecked station as they advanced. The rebuilt stations were constructed of rock-and-adobe and designed like miniature forts. Even the corrals were stone-walled. Armed guards were left at each. J. H. Kelley, a Pony Express rider, and one of the party, related later, "It was no picnic. No amount of money would tempt me to repeat the experience. To begin with, we had to build willow roads, corduroy fashion, across many places along the Carson River

. . . the mosquitoes were so thick it was difficult to tell whether a man was black or white. Arriving at the sink of the Carson River, we began the erection of a fort to protect us from the Indians . . . we next built a fort at Sand Springs, twenty miles from Carson Lake, and another at Cold Springs, thirty-seven miles east of Sand Springs. Here I was assigned to duty as assistant station keeper, under Jim McNaughton. The war against the Pai-Ute was then at its height, and as we were in the middle of their country, it became necessary for us to keep a standing guard, day and night. The Indians were often skulking around, but none of them ever came near enough for us to get a shot at them. Later on we saw the Indian campfires on the mountain and in the morning many tracks. They evidently intended to stampede our horses and if necessary kill us. Next day one of our riders came into camp with a bullet hole through him, having been shot by Indians coming down from Edwards Creek. He was tenderly cared for, but died. As I was lightest man, I was ordered to take his place. I expected to have trouble in Quaking Ash Bottom, where the branches came together from either side, just above my head when mounted. It was impossible for me to see ahead for more than ten or fifteen yards, and it was two miles through the forest. I dropped my bridle reins on the neck of the horse, putting my Sharp's carbine at full cock, keeping both my spurs to the pony's flanks, and he went through that forest like a streak of greased lightning.

"At the top of the hill I dismounted to rest my horse, and looking back saw the bushes moving in several places. As there were no cattle or game in that vicinity, I knew the movement to be caused by Indians. Several days after that, two United States soldiers, who were on their way to their command, were shot and killed from the ambush of those bushes. . . ."

At Robert's Creek station, Roberts and his men met Howard Egan, escorted by a large party of United States Dragoons. Egan was working his way to Carson City with the delayed westbound mail. Mailbags were exchanged and each party returned to its own base. This time, fifty Dragoons accompanied Bolivar Roberts and his men. Bands of Indians constantly shadowed both parties.

Although the mail was moving again, Express riders crossing the sagebrush wilderness never knew if they would reach the next station alive, or whether the station would still be standing when they did arrive. But they never faltered.

Tom Flynn rode into Dry Creek station and found a terrified family of immigrants huddled inside. The station keeper had been killed and scalped.

Major Egan, nearing Butte station, heard firing ahead. Slowing down his pony, he eased closer. The buildings were burning. There was no trace of the station keeper and two stock tenders.

Egan, a sturdy Mormon and the oldest man riding for the Pony Express, later reached Schell Creek after sundown, and found his relief stretched on a bunk, an arrow through one leg. The crippled rider reported that the Paiutes were thick along the route. Egan promptly switched ponies and dashed on. The country between was rugged, threaded by narrow canyons. Ahead, Egan saw light reflected on the night sky and guessed that it came from the camp-fires of Paiutes who were waiting to ambush him on both sides of a canyon. There was no way to pass them except by taking a fourteen-mile detour. He whipped out his revolver, spurred his pony and thundered down the canyon, yelling and firing. He hurtled past the startled Indians and rode safely through.

By starlight, Will Fisher and George Perkins, heading eastward from Ruby Valley with delayed mail, rode into another ambush. While guns roared and arrows droned they dashed ahead, bent low over the withers of their frantically-racing ponies. A bullet punched through Fisher's hat and an arrow protruded, quivering, from Perkins' *mochila,* but they rode clear. When they reached Simpson Spring, the end of their run, there was no relief rider waiting. All westbound mail had been stopped at Salt Lake City because of the Paiute trouble.

Perkins kept going with the *mochila.* Changing horses six times, he finally reached Salt Lake City. He had ridden 300 miles.

William Streeter, westbound rider, found the stock missing and James Alcott, the station keeper, dead at Simpson's Park station. Spurring on, he met the eastbound rider, who turned and rode with him. They reached Smith Creek without trouble. Next morning Streeter set out alone for Diamond Spring. On the trail two prospectors joined him. The three mounted men reached Dry Creek. Here the body of Ralph Rosier, the station keeper, lay outside. On the floor of the station sprawled the remains of John Applegate, a stock tender. The other stock tender, "Bolly" Bulwinkle, was missing. At the next station, Streeter learned what had happened.

Things seemed to have quieted down at Dry Creek. That morning, Applegate had started the fire to cook breakfast. Rosier had picked up a bucket and headed for the spring to fill it. Bulwinkle still snored between his blankets.

The sharp spang of a rifleshot reached Applegate's ears, followed by a scream. He jumped to the doorway. Rosier was writhing on the ground, halfway to the spring. Again the hidden rifle belched fire and the bullet tore through Applegate's groin. Si McCandles,

Four Pony Express riders in a formal pose.

who ran a small trading post nearby, heard the shots and dashed across to the station.

Meanwhile, Bulwinkle had sprung out of his bunk and had grabbed a rifle. Without wasting time in talk, he and McCandles dragged the wounded Applegate inside, then piled grain sacks in the doorway. Applegate lay on the ground, in agony from his wound. "Leave me and run for it," he begged. "You'll never be able to hold them off."

"And let them varmints raise your scalp?" retorted Bulwinkle. "Nope, John, we're sticking."

"Then give me a gun," said Applegate.

Thinking that the wounded man was determined to help defend the station, Bulwinkle drew a Dragoon pistol from beneath his belt, cocked it and handed it to Applegate. The wounded man promptly placed the muzzle against his forehead and triggered.

The thunder of the report filled the room. Astounded, Bulwinkle and McCandles could only stand and stare.

No further shots had been fired by their unseen assailants. There was evidence, however, that Paiutes were waiting in the brush around.

"Let's make a run for it," said McCandles.

"After what happened to him?" retorted Bulwinkle, nodding toward Rosier's contorted form, lying outside, the overturned bucket beside him. "They'd peg us just as fast."

"I'm willing to gamble on it."

Bulwinkle shrugged, figuring that he might just as well die one way as another. They hauled the grain sacks clear of the doorway and dashed out. Several shots kicked up dust around their feet but no other attempt was made to stop them.

Panting, they plugged along the trail, headed for Cape Horn station, twelve miles distant. Sharp rocks began to prick through Bulwinkle's sox and he realized that in the excitement he had forgotten to pull on his boots. When he finally limped into Cape Horn his feet were so cut up that he was crippled for a week.

Elijah N. Wilson—remember the bakery?—reached the end of his run to Deep Creek. When he arrived there was no sign of the rider who should have been waiting to carry the *mochila* on. Without pause, Wilson headed for the next station, Willow Springs. Here he found that the rider had been killed on his run. Peter Neece, the station keeper, was uneasy. A party of thirty Indians, he said, was camped nearby. Wilson, his pony jaded, knew he couldn't outrun them, so he decided to remain at Willow Springs. During the afternoon, four Paiutes rode in and asked for something to eat. Neece, anxious to avoid trouble, gave them a 24-lb. sack of flour. They demanded a sack apiece. Neece grabbed the sack of flour back with one hand and snatched out his revolver with the other.

The four Indians backed away before the threat of the gun, mounted and rode off. But as they passed the station corral, they fired so many arrows at a milk cow that, as Neece said, "It looked like a porcupine."

He levelled his gun. Before the Indians could gallop out of range, he killed two of them.

"Now we'll sure have trouble," he told Wilson grimly. "Before sundown, we'll have the whole pack about our ears." Wilson had visions of baking bread all night for hungry Indians, then being baked himself in the morning. "Since we've got to fight," he said, "let's take the fight to them."

He and Neece loaded all the guns they had, crept out into the sagebrush and crawled in the direction of the Paiute camp. With a Winchester and two revolvers apiece, the two waited, concealed in the sage. A band of Paiutes cantered into view.

The two Express Company employees began blazing away. Convinced that the defenders were still in the station and they were being attacked by a new force, the Indians milled around uncertainly. Wilson and Neece continued their rapid fire. The Paiutes wheeled their ponies and fled.

Shortly after, Elijah J. Wilson rode into trouble again. He was sent along the line—Schell Creek, Spring Valley, Antelope Springs —with horses to replace those stolen by the Paiutes. At Spring Valley the two stock tenders invited him to stay over for supper. Just as they were about to eat, they heard the drumming of hooves. They rushed outside in time to see a band of Indians running off the saddle stock. Afoot, the three chased the thieves, firing, Wilson in the lead. An Indian swung around in the saddle and loosed an arrow. It struck Wilson above the left eye, and penetrated deep into his forehead. He dropped, stunned by the impact. His two companions broke off the shaft of the arrow, but the tip remained deeply embedded. Blood from the wound flowed over his face and soaked his shirt. He was unconscious.

Thinking him dead, or dying, the two dragged him beneath a tree and left him. That night they tramped to the next station.

At dawn they rode back to bury Wilson before the Indians found him and lifted his scalp. To their amazement, he was still alive. One carried him back to Antelope Springs, while the other headed for Ruby Valley—a full day's ride—to bring back a doctor.

The doctor removed the arrow tip, decided he could do nothing more, and left. For six days the Express rider lay tossing in delirium, with no attention beyond the rude nursing of the station hands. He refused to die. Here, Howard Egan, Division Superintendent, checking the stations, found him.

Egan insisted that the doctor be brought back. For another twelve days Wilson lay in a stupor. Then he began to mend. Soon he was back on his feet and carrying mail again!

Forever after, Elijah Wilson always wore a hat, indoors and out, to hide the disfiguring scar on his forehead. With all his misadventures, he died in peaceful retirement, at the age of 71. The town of Wilson, Wyoming, was named in his honor.

While the Washoe Indian War was raging, newspapers throughout the country rang with praise for the heroic Express riders who dared death to bring the mail through. The press was especially indignant at the lack of Government aid. "Hundreds of troops are idling their time away in Utah," thundered *The St. Louis Press-Democrat*, "who, if properly distributed along the Pony Express Route, would protect the riders and the valuable property entrusted to their care . . . it is a matter of highest importance that the bold and daring spirits who risk their necks in carrying a sack of letters through the defiles of the mountains, over unbroken prairies and through the rapid rivers which divide us from the Pacific should be protected. If these gallant fellows cannot perform their task unmolested, the Express will have to be abandoned and the whole country affected thereby."

William Russell was in Washington, D.C. His main purpose in launching the Pony Express had been to prove that the Central

Overland Route was far superior to the Southern Overland Route
—the Oxbow. For carrying mail over the Oxbow Route, William
Butterfield had received a $600,000-a-year government subsidy.
And Butterfield's route, meandering through the Southwest, was
760 miles longer than the Central Overland—the Pony Express
route.

Now that his riders had proved that mail could be regularly
carried over the Central Overland Route in less than half the time
—23 days—consumed by Butterfield's red-and-blue Concord stages,
Russell was pressing for a similar subsidy. A bill authorizing this,
for which he had been fighting strenuously, was about to go before
the Senate. Then came the crushing blow—the Paiute trouble
had stopped the Pony Express. The Post Office Department demanded reliable service. Butterfield was giving it, despite the fact
that his stages were often attacked by Comanches and Apaches, the
mail destroyed and the passengers butchered.

Yet the Pony Express had been running only one month and
now not a *mochila* could cross Nevada. Were it not for Butterfield's lumbering stages east, mail would again be cut off from the
West.

Russell's bill was not passed.

Not only had Russell failed to win his coveted subsidy, but the
ravages of the Paiutes cost the Express Company $75,000 for
repairs on looted stations and replacement of stolen horses. The
Express had lost 150 fine ponies, sixteen men, and seven stations.

Bill Russell, however, like his wiry riders, did not know the
meaning of the word "defeat."

"We'll restore service," he said, "and from now on we'll double
it. Mail will be carried *twice* each week."

8

The Long Trail

It is difficult today to picture the United States as it was a century ago. West of the Missouri River stretched the "Great American Desert," later to be called "The Great Plains." This earthy ocean lapped to the Sierra Nevada Mountains in California, 1,800 miles to the west. It was virtually unexplored. Vast herds of buffalo drifted across it, warlike Indian tribes roamed over its swales. Here and there it wrinkled into hills. In what were later to become the states of Wyoming, Utah, Colorado, and Nevada it erupted into rugged mountains.

There were no highways, no telegraph lines, no railroads. The vast expanse was devoid of habitation except for a few isolated trading posts or mining camps. The only settlement of size was Salt Lake City, Utah, founded by the Mormons in 1847.

The historic Overland Trail, best known today as the Oregon Trail, ribboned across this vast expanse. This route has also been

called the Mormon Trail, the California Trail, the Central Overland Trail, Great Salt Lake Trail, Great Platte Trail, and Immigrant Road. The Indians dubbed it "The White-topped Wagon
Road." It was marked only by the ruts of wagon wheels. For
decades trappers and fur traders traversed it. The first immigrant
train ventured along it in 1841. In 1848–9 it was flooded by a
tide of goldseekers surging to California. From 1858 successive
waves of "Pike's Peakers" flowed along it, drawn by more gold
discoveries in Colorado.

Salt Lake City lay roughly halfway along the Trail. Carson City,
in 1860, boasted only 1,200 inhabitants. Two years before, the
future capital of Nevada had been bare sagebrush flat. Abram
Curry, outraged because Mormons in the small settlement of
Genoa demanded $1,000 for a corner lot, vowed he would establish
a town of his own. Close by, he bought a ranch for several
hundred dollars and proceeded to stake out the streets of his
"town." Like Topsy, it grew—and Carson City became the capital
of Nevada.

At the eastern end of the Overland Trail, other trails from
Missouri River towns joined at Fort Kearney, Nebraska. From
there, the main trail wound westward.

The Pony Express route started at St. Joseph, on the Missouri
River, cut across the northeast corner of Kansas, and angled northwest, across prairie dotted with farms, to Fort Kearney. For two
hundred miles west of Fort Kearney, the route followed the North
Platte River to Old Julesburg. Here the Overland Trail forked,
one branch snaking southwest into Colorado, the other continuing
west to California and Oregon.

The Pony Express riders crossed the South Fork of the Platte

River, headed up Lodge Pole Creek, rode along Thirty-Mile Ridge to Mud Springs, and passed Courthouse Rock, Chimney Rock, and Scotts Bluffs to Fort Laramie, Wyoming. From Fort Laramie the route wound over the foothills of the Rocky Mountains, crossed the Continental Divide through South Pass—twenty miles wide!—skirted Fort Bridger and dropped down to Salt Lake City, then known as the City of the Great Salt Lake.

Beyond, it followed Major Chorpenning's ill-fated mail route across western Utah and Nevada to Fort Churchill. Then the route passed through Carson City, crossed the Sierra Nevada Mountains, rounded the southern end of Lake Tahoe, sloped down to Placerville and Sacramento. There it ended. The mail was transferred to a river steamer and carried down the Sacramento River to San Francisco.

The Express riders travelled the grassy plains of Kansas and Nebraska until they reached Fort Kearney. Beyond, to the Rocky Mountains, they rode through dreary, desolate terrain. From the Rockies to Salt Lake City the trail was rugged, twisting through a mountainous region. Beyond Salt Lake, the riders crossed a thirsty, lonely waste, six hundred miles in extent. Westward rose the high wall of the Sierras, whose high passes were storm-wracked and snowbound in winter.

William Russell allowed four days for the mail to reach Salt Lake City from St. Joseph, but six days to cover the span between Salt Lake and San Francisco. Actually, the two distances were almost equal. Russell recognized that the six-hundred-mile stretch across western Utah and Nevada was by far the more arduous route. The further west the Express courier rode, the rougher the trail became—and the greater the danger from Indians.

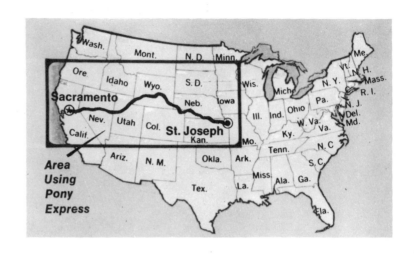

Area
Using
Pony
Express

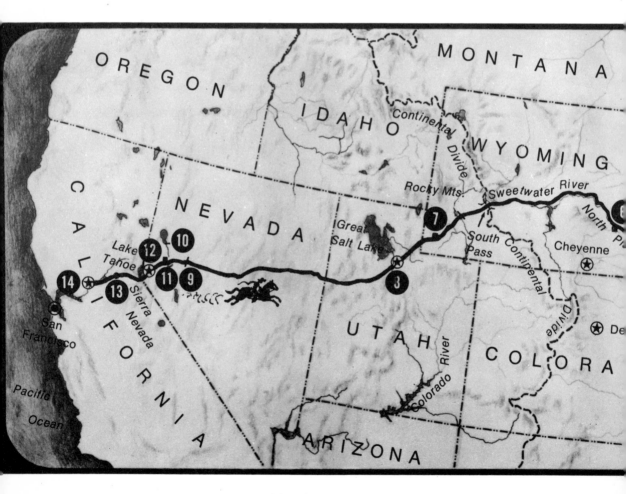

Map showing the Pony Express route from
St. Joseph, Missouri, to Sacramento, California.

1 St. Joseph

2 Big Sandy

3 Fort Kearny (Neb.)

4 Julesburg

5 Chimney Rock

6 Fort Laramie (Wyo.)

7 Fort Bridger

8 Salt Lake City

9 Cold Springs

10 Pyramid Lake (Nev.)

11 Fort Churchill

12 Carson City (Nev.)

13 Placerville

14 Sacramento

In fact, most of the Express route lay through hostile Indian country.

When he left Fort Kearney, heading west, the rider had to be on the alert for trouble. Stages, running from the Missouri River to Salt Lake City were often attacked, the passengers slain and the coaches burned. Immigrant trains were never free from peril.

Beyond Julesburg, the Express rider was liable to tangle with Sioux hunting parties. The Crows also gave trouble, and so did the Shoshones, the Arapahoes, Cheyenne, and the Kiowa.

For three hundred miles the Express route lay across Wyoming. Here were some of the best buffalo grounds of the West. This meant that there were hunting parties from many tribes pursuing buffalo, *and* their greatest enemy, the "paleface." Two Army posts, Fort Laramie and Fort Bridger, could give little protection to travellers beyond their walls.

Then there were the Paiutes in Nevada.

In the beginning, each courier carried a carbine and two revolvers for defense. Many of the riders quickly discarded the carbine because of its weight, and soon most men were only carrying one revolver. Riding alone, they discovered that they just could not afford to fight. However brave a man might be, he stood little chance of defending himself against a furious band of Indians. His best defense was to flee, and his best chance of escape to outrun pursuing Indian ponies. William Russell knew this when he insisted that only the finest and fastest ponies be bought for his riders.

Why were "white men" the victims of such savage Indian attacks? Why did the Indian hate the settler and the Express rider?

For generations, the plains, swarming with buffalo, had been their hunting grounds. In 1841, an immigrant wrote, "I have seen the plains black with them (buffalo) as far as the eye could reach. They seemed to be coming northward continually from the distant plains to the Platte to get water, and would plunge in and swim across it by thousands."

The Indian was dependent on the buffalo. Its flesh gave him meat; its hide provided robes, leggings, tepees, clothing, shields; its bones, fleshing tools, knives, axes, needles; its hooves, glue for feathering arrows; its tail, switches; its horns, ladles, spoons; its sinews, thread. Even its droppings, known to the white immigrant as "buffalo chips," were used as fuel.

The Indian slaughtered just enough buffalo to meet his needs—no more. But when gold was discovered in California, swarms of alien "palefaces" invaded the hunting grounds. It was estimated that in 1849, 8,000 wagons and 30,000 emigrants passed over the Overland Trail. The following year there were even more. The invaders frightened away the game, polluted the waterholes, cut down the scant timber. What was worse, buffalo hunters by the hundred began to slaughter the buffalo for their hides, which sold for $1.75 to $3 apiece. The carcasses were left to rot on the plains. One buffalo hunter, Brick Bond, claimed 1,500 animals in seven days' shooting. He employed five skinners and usually averaged 100 buffalo a day. And he was just one man!

In a three-year period, it was estimated—from the number of hides sold—that over 3,698,000 buffalo were slain.

The prairies were strewn with skeletons of the massive beasts. Years later, homesteaders gathered the bones and sold them to Eastern fertilizer factories. In one year the Santa Fe railroad hauled 7,000,000 pounds.

The Indians were horrified by this wanton slaughter, which to them meant eventual death from starvation. The only solution, was to make war on the "paleface."

Ten Bear, a Comanche chief, revealed the Indian's feelings when he addressed U.S. Treaty Commissioners on Medicine Lodge Creek. In part, he said: "I was born on the prairie, where the wind blew free and there was nothing to break the light of the sun. I was born where there were no enclosures, where everyone drew a free breath. I want to die there, and not within walls. I knew every stream and every wood between the Rio Grande and the Arkansas. I have hunted and lived over that country. I lived like my fathers before me, and like them, I lived happily . . . why do you ask us to leave the rivers and the sun and the wind, and live in houses? Do not ask us to give up the buffalo for the sheep . . . the white man has the country which we loved and we only wish to wander on the prairie until we die."

But there was not much the Indians could do to prevent westward migration. The settlers were determined to cross the prairie, and they used any means they could. One immigrant loaded his camping outfit, blankets and food on a wheelbarrow and set out to push it to California, almost 2,000 miles away. He had covered 250 miles before a kindly wagoner gave him a lift. Another rode across the plains in a little wagon, drawn by two large dogs. There were handcart companies, walking and hauling their possessions in two-wheel carts. At least one "wind wagon" tacked across the plains, a large sail rigged above it. Its wheels were 20 feet in diameter. Finally, it stuck in a deep ravine and was abandoned.

In winter, the Great Plains were impassable for wagons. Immigrants crowded outfitting towns along the Missouri River, buying supplies, fixing their wagons, and waiting for spring. When the grass "greened up" they were assured of food for their teams.

Most of them left in late April or May. Usually, they banded together in trains for protection against Indian attacks. On the canvas sides of many wagons were scrawled such slogans as, "From Suckerdom," "From Pike County," "Ho for California!" "Pilgrim's Progress," "Rough and Ready."

Late starters feared that they might be trapped by winter in the lofty Sierras and share the fate of the Donner party. In the winter of 1846, snow had begun to fall a month earlier than usual. In October, the Donner train had struggled up the rocky canyon of the Truckee. The train was deep in the mountains when winter broke. Oxen and wagons bogged down in twenty-foot snowdrifts. Eighty-one men, women and children were sealed up in icy solitude. Again and again they made desperate efforts to break out. Before relief parties rescued the survivors, thirty-six had died of starvation and exhaustion. Truckee Lake, a sheet of ice near where they were trapped, is now known as Donner Lake.

A wagon train usually travelled 12 to 15 miles a day, and the trip to California took five to six months. There was courtship, marriage, death, birth on the long trail. It was a wearisome journey. The wagons churned up a continuous fog of thick dust. Nerves were often frayed thin by weeks of monotony and danger and trains would split up because of disputes. One husband and wife quarrelled so violently that they cut their wagon in half, making a two-wheel cart out of each part. Then they divided their team, each taking a yoke of oxen.

Another time two men, sharing a wagon, wrangled at Chimney Rock. Each drew his knife and they fought to the death. The victor, weakened by loss of blood, died before his former partner could be buried. They were laid in the same grave.

Most immigrants overloaded their wagons. They did not realize the labor that lay ahead for their teams—the muddy creeks over which the animals would have to struggle, the rocky gullies through which the wagons must be hauled, the grind of months of tortuous travel. After a week or two on the trail, the animals, living on grass, weakened. Sooner or later the day came when the gaunt, bony oxen could haul no further. Then the wagon had to be lightened. One immigrant wrote, "This was a day of scenes of abandoned property; items too numerous to mention; stoves, blacksmith tools, wagons, cooking utensils, provisions of every kind." Another observer reported that the campgrounds at Fort Laramie were strewn with wagon irons, clothing, beans, bacon, pork, miners' washing machinery, log chains, rifles, revolvers.

Many turned back, frightened by Indian attacks, disheartened by deaths in their families, or tired of the everlasting toil behind plodding oxen. Some were just homesick.

But the Pony Express riders covered the Overland Trail from end to end, in ten days.

9

Heroes
on
Horseback

Express riders were tough as rawhide, and they performed incredible riding feats. But there was a limit to what flesh and blood could stand.

Most of the original eighty riders had dropped out, exhausted, before the end of the first year. The riders covered 30–50 miles on a run, which made a round trip of 60–100 miles at top speed once each week. Few men, however tough, could endure the terrific punishment of continuous saddle-pounding. After the Paiute War the mail came through twice weekly—and the riders' work was doubled.

To move the mail even faster, more stations were built and the distance between them was reduced from 15–20 miles to 10–12 miles. Runs, too, were extended until they spanned 60–100 miles, during which the rider, who would cover as much as 400 miles each week, switched mounts up to seven times.

Often, when a courier reached the end of his run, there was no relief rider to carry on the *mochila,* due to sickness or accident. The unwritten law of the Pony Express was that mail had to go through, and the rider hurtled on.

Determined to "deliver," Pony riders made amazing rides. Bob Haslam is credited with the longest—370 miles. Howard Egan once rode 300 continuous miles when his relief failed to appear. Bill James, an eighteen-year-old Virginian, covered 120 miles in less than 10 hours. A nineteen-year-old, Jack Keetley, rode from Big Sandy station in Nebraska Territory, to Elwood, Kansas. Then, finding no relief rider, he doubled back, relaying the mail at Seneca. The distance he rode was 340 miles. He used remounts. Jim Moore, also lacking a relief, rode 140 miles, and repeated the distance on his return trip, 280 miles in all.

The Pony Express rider. Here the artist mistakenly shows the rider with the mail on his back.

Young Bill Cody packed the *mochila* from Red Buttes to Three Crossings, a lonely 75-mile trail. This included the fording of the North Platte River, a half mile wide. The Platte, often swollen and turbulent, took many lives. Reaching Three Crossings, fifteen-year-old Cody found that his relief rider had been killed. He switched ponies and rode on to the next home station, Rocky Ridge, 85 miles. Here he passed the *mochila* on, promptly turned and retraced his route. When he rode into his home station he had covered 322 miles.

Henry Avis made a hair-raising ride from Mud Springs, Nebraska, during a time when the Sioux were raiding all down the line. He succeeded in eluding the Indians and reached Horseshoe Creek, the end of the run, without trouble. There was no relief rider at Horseshoe. A stage pulled in and the driver reported a large war party of Sioux near Deer Creek, the next home station. Avis decided to carry the *mochila* on.

The station keeper protested. "You loco, Hank?" he demanded. "The Injuns'll raise your scalp, for sure."

The trail crossed a succession of rolling hills. Every time Avis approached the crest of a hill, he dismounted, led his pony and carefully searched the country ahead for signs of the Sioux. At Deer Creek he found the station keeper and stock tenders forted up. The Sioux had drive off all the livestock, including the ponies. But the delayed rider from the east galloped in. Avis surrendered the *mochila,* turned his pony and headed back to Mud Springs. When he arrived he'd been dodging Indians for sixteen hours and had covered 210 miles.

The riders often passed each other on the trail.

Jim Moore's run was from Midway station, Nebraska, to Julesburg, a 280-mile round trip. He shared it with another rider. The two crisscrossed, each carrying a *mochila* one way.

When he came within half a mile of a relay station, Moore was in the habit of giving a "coyote yell," so that the stock tender could have a pony waiting, ready rigged.

"As easy as it may seem," he said, "few men are able to stand the pounding they receive forking a racing horse over a 140-mile route."

Once when he stepped out of the saddle at Julesburg, thankful to reach the end of his run, he found his relief lying on a bunk, burning up with fever. He had hoped to snatch a few hours sleep, but he couldn't let the *mochila* lie there. So he hastily swallowed a mug of coffee, stuffed some cold meat into a pocket and stepped into the saddle again for another 140-mile ride. When he rode into Midway, twenty-two hours after he had left it, he'd covered

280 miles. Later, the Express Company gave him a gold watch to express its thanks.

"When I look back," said Jay Kelley, who had many narrow escapes during the Paiute War, "I wonder that we were not all killed. There were only four men at each station and the Paiutes were roaming all over the country, in bands of thirty to forty, looking for trouble. Yet I had my most narrow escape from death one evening after sundown when I rode past an immigrant train. One fellow raised his rifle and shot at me—pointblank. I was moving fast, but that slug whined mighty close. On my return trip I caught up with the train and asked how come they were gunning for Express riders. A gent steps forward, kinder sheepish, and said he thought I was an Indian."

During the Civil War, which broke out the following year, Kelley became a captain in the First Nevada Infantry. He survived the war, returned to Nevada, and became a miner.

"Pony Bob" Haslam, one of the most daring of the Express riders, told of the outbreak of the Paiute War. "Virginia City," he relates, "was hourly expecting an attack from the hostile Indians. A stone hotel on C Street was in course of construction and had reached an elevation of two stories. This was hastily transformed into a fort for the protection of women and children. From the city, the signal fires of the Paiutes could be seen on every mountain peak. All available men and horses were pressed into service to repel the impending assault."

The Paiutes never attacked Virginia City but they did sack many of the Express stations, among them Smith's Creek. "The whites," Haslam recalled, "were well protected in the shelter of a stone house, from which they fought the savages for four days.

At the end of that time they were relieved by the appearance of about fifty volunteers from Cold Springs. These men reported that they had buried the station keeper, John Williams, but when they found the body it was almost devoured by wolves.

"When I arrived at the Sink of the Carson, I found the station men badly frightened, but well-armed and ready for a fight. Fifty warriors, decked out in their war paint, were skulking around."

Bob Haslam was one of the few men who stuck with the Pony Express from start to finish. When a telegraph line was strung across the Continent and the "Pony" went out of business, Haslam headed for Idaho. Here he rode a 100-mile Express route with one horse. When the Modoc War broke out, he rode past the bodies of ninety Chinese along the trail, all blackening in the sun. They had been slaughtered by ravaging Modoc Indians.

This was too much for Haslam, and he quit. His successor, Sye Macaulas, was killed by the Indians on his first run.

Haslam bought a Flathead Indian pony and rode to Salt Lake City, 400 miles away. His brother-in-law, the United States Marshal for Utah, appointed him a deputy. He found law enforcement dull, quite and became a Wells, Fargo stagecoach messenger on the Salt Lake-Denver run. He rode the 720-mile route for several years, guarding the familiar green Wells, Fargo strong boxes from hold-up men and Indians. Years later, he died peacefully in Chicago, an old man.

Bill Campbell was a bullwhacker—ox team driver—for Russell, Majors and Waddell, who ran the Pony Express. He tried hard to become a "Pony" rider, but failed. He topped six feet and weighed 140 lbs. The Express Company wanted small, wiry men. The lighter their burdens, the faster the ponies travelled.

With winter, however, Campbell's chance came. "The boys were dropping out pretty fast," he recalled. "They couldn't stand the strain of constant riding. When winter came, the job was too much for them. My relay was along the Platte, between Fort Kearney and Cottonwood Springs, one hundred miles to the west. I changed ponies four times, at Plum Creek, Pat Mullaly's, Midway and Gilman Ranch. The hardest ride I ever had was when I had to spend twenty-four hours in the saddle, carrying the *mochila* 120 miles to Fairfield. It was midwinter. The temperature was down to zero. My horse could barely make five miles an hour through the heavy snow. Often I had to get down and lead him. The only way I kept on the trail was by watching the tall weeds, which showed above the snowdrifts. When I reached Fort Kearney I was so worn out I could scarcely sit the saddle. There was no relief to carry on the mail. I threw the *mochila* over a fresh pony and started for the next station, twenty miles ahead. I reached there at four o'clock in the afternoon, just twenty-four hours from the time I started."

Campbell passed the *mochila* on, but was too exhausted to ride back. He stretched out on a bunk in the station and returned to Fort Kearney on the stage the next day. "With a four-mule team," he said, "the stage took four days to cover the run I made in twenty-four hours."

Campbell found that the greatest danger on the trail was the vast buffalo herds. Countless thousands of the shaggy beasts drifted through western Nebraska. "If a man rode into a herd he was a goner—he never got out alive."

Packs of wolves followed the buffalo, trying to tear down the calves. "One night I saw fifteen or twenty wolves clustered around a horse they had killed. The pack followed me to the next station.

"It was midwinter and the temperature was down to zero."

Every time they got too close I'd toot my horn and they'd pull back. Later, I doctored the carcass of that dead horse with strychnine. When I passed again, I found twelve dead wolves lying around the bait."

On one trip, Campbell's pony stepped into a badger hole, throwing him over its head, dragging the *mochila* with him. When Campbell regained his feet, the pony had bolted. He shouldered the *mochila* and started to walk to the next station through the night. A stage approached from the opposite direction. Tied to its boot was the runaway. It had galloped on, following the familiar route, checked, and had run with the stage team. The driver had secured it. Campbell thankfully remounted and continued his run.

Bill Cates, another rider who stuck with the Pony Express from beginning to end, tells how he almost lost his scalp. "The Kiowas were on the rampage. One day about three hundred of them in full war regalia took after me. I knew what those war bonnets meant and I went all out. But some of the Kiowas forked as good horseflesh as I did. They began to gain on me. Usually, the commandant of Fort Riley, about the time I was due, sent a detachment out to meet me. I knew that if they skipped this time I was through. Was I thankful when I saw the escort closing in ahead! The Indians swerved away and fled. I kept my scalp!"

Tom King, a young Mormon boy, had a Utah run. "My longest ride," he tells, "was from Salt Lake City to Ham's Fork, 145 miles. It took thirteen hours. Many a time I went to sleep in the saddle and the pony would keep up its pace. Other riders would sleep, too. One night I rode into Bear River, after an eighty-mile ride from Salt Lake, and reported to the station keeper that I had not seen Henry Worley, who was riding in the opposite direction.

Bill Campbell, Pony
Express rider.

Bill Cates. Starting from St.
Joseph with Lincoln's
Inaugural Address, he made
the fastest trip in the
history of the Pony Express.

Worley reported the same thing about me at the other station. We had both been sound asleep in our saddles when we passed."

Special efforts were made by the "Pony" to rush news of national importance to the Pacific Coast. One of the most crucial "specials" was that which carried President Lincoln's inaugural message on March 4, 1861. War or peace between North and South might depend upon that message.

The long chain of riders was as eager to beat the record as they had been with news of Lincoln's election, November 7, 1860, which reached the Coast in six days, seventeen hours. Right along the line, division superintendents had been told that the Inaugural Message must go through at utmost speed, sparing neither rider nor horses.

Across the plains, bitter weather delayed the couriers. Snow lay thick over much of the route. Storms raged in the Sierras. Ponies floundered through snowdrifts, or dropped, dead from exhaustion. Riders had to be lifted half-frozen from their saddles at relay stations.

Bill Cates carried the message 75 miles through the bleak storm-swept hills of Wyoming. "It was tough," said Cates. "The closer we approached the mountains, the worse conditions got. We had the best horses. We rode them to death."

Seven days passed before the message reached Salt Lake City. Five days later, Fort Churchill, Nevada, from which a telegraph line ran to San Francisco, reported the message had arrived. The time was twelve days. Crossing the Sierras, the Express rider's mount bogged down in deep snow. He left the pony, donned snowshoes and pressed on afoot, carrying the *Mochila*. For thirteen miles he struggled through the snow. Finally, frostbitten, he crawled into Strawberry station on his hands and knees.

Ras Egan's horse slipped on ice, fell and broke its neck. Young Egan threw the *mochila* over his shoulder and toiled five miles through the snow to Camp Floyd.

How many Californians, reading Lincoln's message in the comfort of their homes, realized that the heroic struggle of the "Pony" riders across the continent had brought it to them? They took it for granted that the Pony Express would deliver.

It always did.

Travelling by stage, Mark Twain met an Express rider and told about it in *Roughing It*.

"All interest was taken in stretching our necks and watching for the 'Pony-rider'—the fleet messengers who sped across the continent from St. Joe to Sacramento, carrying letters 1,900 miles in 8 days. The pony-rider was usually a little bit of a man, brimful of spirit and endurance. No matter what time of day or night his watch came on, and no matter whether it was winter or summer, raining, snowing, hailing or sleeting, or whether his 'beat' was a level straight road or a crazy trail over mountain crags and precipices, or whether it led through peaceful regions or regions that swarmed with hostile Indians, he must always be ready to leap into the saddle and be off like the wind . . . he came crashing up to the station where stood two men, holding a fast, impatient steed, the transfer of rider and mailbag was made in the twinkling of an eye, and away flew the eager pair. Both rider and horse went 'flying light.' The rider's dress was thin and fitted close; he wore a 'roundabout' and a skull cap, and tucked his pantaloons into his boot tops like a race rider . . . his horse was stripped of all unnecessary weight, too. He wore a little wafer of a riding saddle, and no visible blanket . . . the stage-coach travelled about a hundred to one hundred and twenty-five miles a day (twenty-four hours) the

The trip across the Rockies was difficult and very dangerous.

pony-rider about 250. There were about eighty pony riders in the saddle all the time, night and day, stretching in a long procession from Missouri to California, forty flying eastward and forty westward, making 400 gallant horses earn a stirring livelihood.

"Here he comes! Every neck is stretched further and every eye strained wider. Away across the dead level of the prairie a black spot appears against the sky, and it is plain that it moves. Well, I should think so! In a second or two it becomes a horse and rider, rising and falling, rising and falling—sweeping toward us nearer and nearer—growing more and more distinct, more and more sharply defined—nearer and nearer still, and the flutter of the hoofs comes faintly to the ear—another instant and a whoop and a hurrah from our upper deck, a wave of the rider's hand, but no reply, and man and horse burst past our excited faces and go swinging away like the belated fragment of a storm. So sudden is it all, and so like a flash of unreal fancy, that but for the flake of white foam left quivering and perishing on a mail sack after the vision had flashed by and disappeared, we might have doubted whether we had seen any actual horse and man at all, maybe."

A letter to Abraham Lincoln, sent via Pony Express.

10

Rough and Ready

The station keepers and stock tenders were the unsung heroes of the Pony Express. The stations that stretched from the Missouri River to Sacramento, California, were vital links in a chain. The flying Express riders depended on them for remounts and shelter. When the chain was broken, as it was for three weeks during the Nevada Paiute War, service came to a halt.

While the more spectacular exploits of the Express riders thrilled the nation, the bravery of the station keepers and stock tenders received little notice. Yet they were a sturdy breed. True, they were tough men. They had to be. They were bearded, dirty, and "whiffy," too. Usually, the scarcity of water made bathing impossible. Their blankets were never washed and were alive with lice. When the vermin became unbearable the men stripped and spread their shirts, pants and vests over an anthill. The swarming ants ate the lice, and the clothes were donned until next "washday."

Often station hands never saw a human being beyond the teamster who drove the monthly supply wagon from the "home" station and—twice weekly—the Express rider who dashed up and was gone in a flash. When they saw Indians, they grabbed their rifles and hoped for the best. For all this, they were paid as little as $30 a month.

The further the route snaked westward, the more primitive the stations became. In Kansas, at the eastern end of the trail, some stations were located at ranches. At Cottonwood, for instance, the Hollenberg Ranch was a "home" station. This was one of the most comfortable stations on the route. George H. Hollenberg, a native of Germany, had formerly been a prospector who had wandered over California, Australia, and Peru. He had been shipwrecked off the Florida coast; his health had failed and he had decided to settle down. He and his wife Sophie built a cabin on the Oregon Trail.

Here he opened a trading post which supplied the needs of passing immigrant trains. Hollenberg station, as it became known, gained a reputation for serving good meals. Stages, immigrants, and teamsters began to use it as a stopover.

Hollenberg built a rambling ranchhouse and hired clerks to handle the trade. His ranch became a stage stop and Post Office. The six Pony Express employees stationed there slept in the spacious attic and generally lived well.

Another popular "home" station was Sportsman's Hall, founded by John Blair, a Scotsman, and located on the western slope of the

Hollenberg Ranch, Pony Express "home" station in Washington County, Kansas.

Sierra Nevada Mountains in California. Blair had come west with the goldseekers. He had decided, however, that there were more convenient ways of making a living than digging. He found a level spot on the rugged trail that led up to the Sierras and built a solid, two-story hostelry, using the stately pines that grew nearby for lumber. Sportsman's Hall was so large that it could sleep and feed a hundred guests. Every night it was crowded with stagecoach passengers, teamsters, prospectors. A huge stable sheltered their animals. Twice it burnt down, and twice Blair rebuilt it.

At the other extreme, Dugway, a station in Utah, was described by a traveller as "a hole, four feet deep, roofed over with split cedar trunks, and with a rough adobe chimney. Water had to be brought in casks." Commenting upon food at the station, the same traveller wrote, "diet is sometimes reduced to 'wolf mutton' or a little boiled wheat or rye, their drink is brackish water."

The names of some stations suggest they were not much better: Sulphur Springs, Joe's Dugout, Needle Rock, Muddy Creek, Rocky Ridge, Split Rock, Red Buttes, Chimney Rock, Sand Hill, Log Chain, Kiowa, Lone Tree, River Bed, Canyon, Cape Horn, Dry Creek, Sink of the Carson, Point Lookout.

Food at most stations was plain. The monthly supply wagon usually brought bacon, flour, dried fruits, beans, molasses, corn-meal, coffee. As we have seen, station keepers baked their own bread.

Rations for the men might run short, but never hay and grain for the horses. They were always well fed. They *had* to be kept in prime condition.

The common dessert throughout the pioneer West, and at many stations, was dried-apple pie. Too often this was the only dessert ever served and the men yearned for a little variety. One station keeper expressed his feelings in verse:

> *"I loathe! Abhor! Detest! Despise!*
>   *Abominate dried-apple pie;*
> *I like good bread; I like good meat,*
>   *Or anything that's good to eat;*
> *But of all poor grub beneath the skies*
>   *The poorest is dried-apple pies.*
> *Tread on my corns, or tell a lie*
>   *But please don't pass the dried-apple pie."*

There was little to relieve the drab monotony of life at the more remote sections. Any occurrence that held a glimmer of humor was eagerly talked about. A traveller dropped into one such station and was invited to eat. He pulled up a three-legged stool, and the station keeper set a chunk of fat pork and a jar of mustard on the plank table.

"Excuse me, but I never eat pork," said the traveller politely.

"Wal, help yourself to the mustard," returned the station keeper.

"Help yourself to the mustard," became a favorite saying all down the line.

Stations were placed at varied distances so that the ponies could span them without slackening speed. In broken country they might be ten miles or less apart; on flat prairie up to fifteen miles. At "home" stations, where the Express riders ate and slept, there were two to four stock tenders, in addition to the station keeper. The "home" stations also carried supplies for a string of four to seven relay stations stretching away on either side.

Mark Twain described a typical "home" station:

"The roof was thatched and sodded with a thick layer
of earth, and from this sprung a pretty rank growth of
weeds and grass. It was the first time we had seen a man's
garden on the top of his house. The buildings consisted
of barns, stable-room for 12 or 15 horses and a hut as
eating room for passengers. This latter had bunks in it
for the station keeper and a hostler or two. You could
rest your elbow on its eaves, and you had to bend to get
in at the door. In place of a window there was a square
hole about large enough for a man to crawl through, but
this had no glass in it. There was no stove, but the fireplace served all needful purposes. There were no shelves,
no cupboards, no closets. In a corner stood an open sack
of flour and nestling against its base were a couple of
black and venerable tin coffee pots, a tin teapot, a little
bag of salt and a side of bacon . . . the table was a greasy
board on stilts, and the tablecloth and napkins had not
come—and they were not looking for them either."

Relay stations were even more crude—often no more than a
hut and rough stable. The two men occupying them took care of
two or three ponies and prepared one for riding when the Express
rider dashed up.

Station buildings were of every type, depending upon their
location. On the desert they were usually built of adobe bricks.
In mountainous country, rock was used, or a hole was dug in the
hillside. Little Muddy was built of loose stone and set in a treeless
canyon. The view from Point Lookout was a stretch of parched
desert, with rugged mountain ranges silhouetted against the hori-

zon. Butte was another rock structure, chinked with mud, some thirty feet long. The rear end of a wagon box, chipped by bullets, served as door, and the interior was divided by a canvas partition. On one side of the canvas were two bunks, with harness, sacks of wheat, meal and potatoes piled underneath them. The other "room" boasted a huge fireplace. A spring welled out of the earth in one corner. The furnishings were a plank table, three-legged stools and log benches. Clothing, spurs, rifles and revolvers hung from pegs driven into the walls. A tin bucket, a wash basin, and a tin dipper sat on a shelf beside the door.

The entire route of the Pony Express was divided into six divisions, each managed by a superintendent. Benjamin J. Ficklin supervised the entire operation.

The superintendents spent most of their time riding from station to station, checking on the livestock, hiring men, rebuilding stations sacked by Indians, and recovering stolen horses. In short, their job was to keep the mail moving smoothly.

Although every Express Company employee took an oath which, in part, declared: "I will not quarrel or fight with any other employees of the firm," tempers sometimes flared, when strong-willed men were penned together for months on isolated stations. Nerves frayed raw by the threat of Indian attack, the men were liable to lash out. With the type of men who were willing to suffer the risk and hardships of station life, impulse often led to action.

On July 12, 1861, at Rock Creek station, J. B. Hickok, a stock tender, wiped out David McCandles, James Woods, and James Gordon in a blazing gunfight that exploded after an argument. Hickok, a lanky twenty-three-year-old, was later to become famous as "Wild Bill" Hickok, gunman and frontier marshal.

Once, Montgomery Maze, an Express rider, rode into Smith's Creek, westbound. For some reason his mount was not ready. Maze, irritated by the delay, expressed his opinion of H. Trumbo, the station keeper, in strong language. Trumbo pulled out his pistol, aimed it at the indignant rider, and pulled the trigger. There was no more than a metallic click. The gun was not loaded, and Trumbo probably knew it. But Maze didn't!

The following day Maze retraced his route with the eastbound *mochila*. He carried a rifle. Without warning, he levelled on Trumbo and fired. The slug struck Trumbo on the hip, inflicting a dangerous wound. He dropped to the ground and lay writhing. Two stock tenders packed him into the station. Later, he died. Maze had both stock tenders sign a statement that Trumbo threatened him. Later, the rider was arrested and charged with murder. The testimony of the stock tenders, however, cleared him.

Occasionally, the Express Company made contracts with hunters to supply relay stations with fresh meat. One of these hunters was Bob Jennings, a sullen, grizzly-bear of a man, over six feet, with a shock of sandy hair and an uncertain temper. He was a poker player, too, and a poor loser.

One afternoon Jennings brought meat to the station near Fort Laramie, Wyoming, run by "Hod" Russell. Hod was a slightly-built, inoffensive fellow who loved to play poker. Hod promptly produced a dog-eared deck of cards and the two sat down to play. By sundown, Jennings had lost $100. He refused to pay, claiming that Hod cheated. Several men standing around backed the station keeper. Jennings finally paid, under protest. He left the station in an ugly mood.

Two days later, Hod climbed up to the seat of a stage to chat with the driver while the four-mule team was changed. A gun roared. Hod pitched forward, thudded down to the ground—dead. There was no sign of the killer except for a puff of white smoke curling above the brush, fifty yards away.

Jennings was immediately suspect. The commandant at Fort Laramie sent a detachment of soldiers out to round him up. But Jennings knew every foot of the rugged terrain and eluded them.

Hod Russell was buried and the affair forgotten, except by Robert Spotswoode, Division Superintendent. Spotswoode, called in "Buffalo Bill" Comstock, so called because he hunted buffalo to feed the soldiers at the fort. Comstock was a rugged, hardy man, whose high cheekbones denoted a strain of Indian blood. Spotswoode, offered him a reward if he would bring in Jennings, dead or alive.

Comstock and three of his partners disguised themselves as Indians. Hunting and fishing, they drifted around the country until they discovered that the fugitive had built himself a brush wickiup in an isolated area, and was hiding out. They knew Jennings was a deadly shot and in a mood to cut down anyone on sight. When they sauntered into his camp, he raised his rifle uncertainly, put it down when his visitors made the peace sign. They squatted by the fire, talking to each other in Sioux. Jennings set his rifle aside and began to broil an antelope steak. The four flung themselves upon him. Though he fought savagely, he was finally made prisoner. Heading for the Overland Trail, they stopped a stage and loaded Jennings in the rear boot, his arms and legs bound. They rode behind the stage as escort. The prisoner was delivered to the commandant at Fort Laramie—and promptly hanged. Justice was swift in the Old West!

But these were isolated incidents. On the whole, Express riders and station men were friendly, hardworking and law-abiding.

Quarrels might occasionally erupt, but killings were few.

Then there were men like Johnny Frey, a wiry, daredevil rider and a favorite with the ladies. His run lay between St. Joseph and Seneca, Kansas. It crossed smiling farm country, dotted with prosperous ranches. When Johnny dashed along the trail he had a handwave and a yell for every goodlooking girl. Miss Betty Hobbs, who taught in the little schoolhouse at Syracuse, always ran to the door and waved as he drummed past. She claimed she could check the clock by Johnny. On "pony day" he was always right on time.

He never failed to toot his horn when he neared one farmhouse, occupied by the buxom widow Brawn and her four red-cheeked daughters. As he swept past, one of the daughters always stood beside the trail, holding homemade cakes and cookies. Johnny snatched what he could, reining down a trifle, but the cookies always seemed to slip through his fingers. Then one of the young ladies had an idea—she would make her cookies with a hole in the center so that Johnny could hook a finger through as he galloped by.

Thus, it is claimed, the doughnut was born!

Another feminine admirer of Johnny's coveted the flaming red bandana that he knotted around his neck. She was anxious to sew it into a quilt. Every time he passed, she begged for the bandana—in vain. Finally, she saddled her own pony, and waited. When he pounded along the trail, she spurred her own mount, dropped in beside him, and made a grab for the red bandana.

Johnny spurred ahead and she missed. Desperately, she grabbed his shirttail, and ripped off a strip. This she carried home with glee, and sewed *that* into her quilt.

11

Buffalo Billy

The most famous Pony Express rider was also the youngest.

Long before most boys graduate from grammar school, young "Buffalo Billy" Cody was a seasoned plainsman and Indian fighter. Living was rough in Kansas Territory when his father homesteaded in Salt Creek Valley, and Billy showed his mettle early. Once, when an older boy beat him in school, ten-year-old Cody slashed the bully with a bowie knife. The boy's father demanded Billy's arrest. Billy eluded his pursuers, joined a wagon train and left for a forty-day trip to Fort Kearney. His job was handling the cavvyard—a herd of spare oxen. The "smart, dirty-faced kid" became a favorite with the bullwhackers.

One night, young Cody saw the headdress of an Indian protruding above the squat brush. The intruder was crawling up to the camp. The boy lined the sights of his gun on the slinking form and fired. The shot roused the camp. News quickly spread that "little Billy" had "killed an Indian stone-dead." Later, *The Leavenworth Times* hailed him as "the youngest Indian killer on the plains."

The youngster had another narrow escape on this trip. The wagonmaster set out for a train ahead, taking young Cody and a man named Woods with him. A band of Indians jumped them in a ravine. Yelling, the painted braves circled them. There was no escape. Simpson, the wagonmaster, quickly shot the three mules they were riding, and dragged them into a triangle, using their carcasses as a makeshift barricade. The Indians charged, loosing arrows, one of which pierced Woods' shoulder. The three repelled them with single-shot rifles and repeating pistols.

Again the Indians charged and again were driven off, leaving several dead lying on the ground. The Indians tried to set fire to the grass, but it was too short to burn.

When night came, the three dug into the ground with their knives to gain more cover. At dawn the Indians charged again. Just then, however, the sharp crack of bull whips sounded through the ravine. Their wagon train wound into the ravine and the Indians fled.

That fall, young Cody tried trapping. With Dave Harrington, aged twenty-three, he set out for the Republican River. The two took a wagon, hauled by a span of oxen, traps and supplies.

On Praire Dog Creek, deep in Indian country, they built a dug-out. One ox had died, and the other had been mauled by a bear. Then Billy slipped on the ice and broke a leg. His companion splinted and bound the leg, and left the boy in the dugout with their supplies, fixing a can on a stick so that Billy could reach outside and scrape up snow for water. Then he set out afoot for the nearest settlement, a ten-day journey, to acquire another span of oxen to haul Billy and the wagon out.

For over a week, the crippled boy lay in the dugout undisturbed. Then the brush in the entrance was swept aside and an Indian's paint-daubed face thrust in. The dugout quickly filled with Indians. They took Billy's rifle, pistol, cooking utensils and most of his food, but spared his life. All they left was part of a deer, flour, salt, and baking powder. On this the boy lived for two weeks. Deep snow now covered the dugout. Harrington, back with two oxen, only located Billy by his feeble shouts. Lying in the wagon bed, the boy endured a jolting ten-day journey to a ranchhouse, where Harrington had borrowed the oxen.

After that, Billy went buffalo hunting, rode messenger between freight trains, and prospected for gold in the Pike's Peak region. He was no novice when Joseph Slade hired him as a Pony Express rider at the age of fifteen.

His run was through dangerous country. "Along the trail," he relates, "Indians were often lying in wait for passing stages and 'Pony' riders. We had to take many chances running the gauntlet."

Because the Indians stole so many Express ponies, Slade, the division superintendent, decided to gather a party of Express riders, stock tenders and stage drivers to go after them. Young Cody was included. It was thought that the stolen ponies had been driven to the head of the Powder River. Slade's party followed.

On Horse Creek they found tracks of shod ponies. The trail led to Crazy Woman's Fork. Here the sign indicated that another band of Indians had joined those fleeing with the stolen horses.

Slade's party was now in hostile Indian country. It pushed ahead cautiously. Beyond Clear Creek they sighted an Indian camp and the stolen ponies grazing with the horse herd nearby. Never suspecting the white men would follow so far into their country, the Indians had left no scouts out.

Outnumbered three to one, the pursuers decided to wait for darkness, when they would charge, open fire and stampede the horse herd. The plan was a complete success. Before the astonished Indians could grasp what was happening, the yelling riders had thundered right through their camp and run the horse herd off. They drove the ponies south. Four days later, they reached the Overland Trail. In addition to recovering the Express ponies, they had taken around 100 Indian ponies.

The Indian ponies were equally divided, and the victorious Express employees and stage drivers proceeded to celebrate. To quote young Cody, "There seemed to be no limit to the carousing." Slade had a drunken quarrel with a stage driver and shot him.

On another occasion, young Cody went hunting. Beating through the back country, he came upon a number of horses grazing beside a creek. Beyond, on the slope of a hill, he saw a dugout, with a wooden door. The door was closed and light shone beneath it.

Billy decided it must be a party of trappers. Always cautious, he concealed his pony in the brush, with the sage hens he had killed hanging from the saddle horn. Then he tramped up the hillside and banged on the door.

. When it opened, he almost collapsed from shock. Packed in the dugout, playing cards, were eight notorious outlaws who had been murdering, robbing and stealing horses throughout the country.

"What do you want, youngster?" demanded the leader.

"Nothing, just figured on getting acquainted," said Cody. "I was hunting and I saw your horses."

"Where's your cayouse?"

"I left him in the brush."

"Jim and Whitey, you go get the critter," the leader told two of his men. Cody's heart sank. Without his horse he'd be helpless. He concealed his feelings and grinned. "Sure," he said.

He led the two to his saddled pony, and lifted the sage hens off the horn. One outlaw grasped the pony's bridle and led it in the direction of the dugout. Cody followed, the other man at his heels.

The young Express rider had a feeling that if he ever entered that dugout he'd never leave it alive. These hardened killers could not afford to let him live to reveal their hideout.

"It was now quite dark," he relates. "I had both of my revolvers with me. I dropped one of the sage hens. When the man behind me bent to pick it up, I pulled out one of the Colts and hit him hard on the back of the head. He fell senseless. The man ahead turned to see what was wrong. Before he could fire I shot him dead in his tracks."

Hearing gunfire, the remaining outlaws rushed out of the dugout, but they could see nothing in the darkness. Astride his pony, young Cody was heading across country, back to Horseshoe station.

At one time there was a rumor that the Express riders transported large sums of money in their *cantinas.* Several riders were intercepted and one was killed by renegades. Buffalo Billy had a notion that his turn would come. He cut a saddle blanket in the same shape as the *mochila* and sewed old saddle pouches in each corner. He made a practice of throwing this over the regular *mochila*.

He was not unduly surprised when two men rose from behind rocks ahead when he galloped through a narrow canyon on his run. Both men held levelled rifles. He reined in.

"We don't want you, boy," said one outlaw, as they stepped up to him. "Just toss us the Express pouches."

Young Cody swung to the ground, grabbed the fake *mochila* and swung it at the outlaw. It dropped and the man bent to retrieve it. As he did so, Cody drew a revolver and fired at the other man across his pony's back. The slug shattered the renegade's right arm. He dropped his rifle and staggered backward.

Cody vaulted into the saddle and charged at the man picking up what he thought was the *mochila*. The pony bowled him over and the young Express rider spurred on. As he pounded away, the outlaw scrambled to his feet, grabbed his rifle and began firing. Billy escaped unhurt.

Later, both outlaws were captured and hanged.

A burly prospector once stood eyeing fifteen-year-old Billy. "You're a mighty small feller to take on a job like this," he commented.

"Maybe so," replied Cody, and jerked out his Colt revolver, "but I got a notion this makes me just as big as you."

In 1864, at the age of eighteen, Buffalo Billy enlisted in the Union Army. The Civil War was raging. Mustered out at war's end, he married, but he was too restless to settle down.

He became a scout for the Army, and the stories of his exploits on various Indian campaigns would fill volumes. For bravery in a skirmish with Indians on the Loup River, Nebraska, "Mr. Cody" was awarded the Congressional Medal of Honor on May 22, 1872. He was then twenty-six years old.

His knife duel with Yellow Hand, a young chief, in the Cheyenne campaign, drew headlines in newspapers throughout the country. Cody was scouting through the hills, in advance of a detachment of troopers of the Fifth Cavalry. Suddenly he came face to face with a band of Southern Cheyenne Indians. At their head was a muscular young chief, Yellow Hand.

Both the chief and Cody fired. Cody's bullet bored through the Indian's leg and killed his pony. At that moment, Cody's mount stepped into a badger hole and went down, too. Yellow Hand fired again and missed. Cody kicked free of his pony. Colt revolver in one hand and knife in the other, he rushed at the chief. Yellow Hand was on his feet, too—waiting. Cody fired again. The bullet struck the Indian in the chest. He reeled. Then Cody was at him and drove his knife to Yellow Hand's heart. In seconds, he had torn off the Indian's war bonnet and had scalped him. By now the troopers had rushed up, and the Cheyenne fled. One trooper yelled, "The first scalp for Custer!"

Paid off as an Army scout in November, 1872, Cody entered a new field, acting. His first appearance was in a play, "The Scouts of the Prairie." For the next few years he spent the summers on the plains, leading hunting parties or scouting in various Indian campaigns. He spent the rest of the year touring the eastern states, appearing in a number of melodramas.

By now he was a national figure. A legion of newspaper and magazine stories, extolling his prowess, appeared. So, too, did the never-ending series of "Buffalo Bill" dime novels—over 550 in all —with fanciful titles, such as *Buffalo Bill's Buckskin Braves, Buffalo Bill's Red Trail, Buffalo Bill's Death Charm.*

In 1885 he launched the "Wild West Show" which was to make him famous throughout the United States and Europe. Combining trick shooters, Indians, scouts, stagecoaches, daredevil riders, it drew capacity crowds everywhere it was held. Two years later he took the show to England. Again it was a smashing success. A command performance was given for Queen Victoria.

His shows travelled for years. Money poured into his pockets— and poured out just as fast. In 1910 his receipts exceeded $1,000,000. Naturally a gambler, he speculated—and lost. He gave lavishly to relatives and friends, to anyone with a "hard luck" story. Aging, he lost control of his show. Finally, he was reduced to such want that he applied for the $10-a-month pension which he believed went with the Medal of Honor.

The Adjutant-General wrote back that the medal was only awarded to members of the United States Army. Since he had received it as a civilian scout, "Mr. Cody's" name had been stricken from the records.

Buffalo Bill died in Denver, on January 10, 1917, a man in his seventies. His body lay in state in the rotunda of the Capitol, and 25,000 people filed past it to pay their respects. He was buried on the summit of Lookout Mountain, near Denver.

"Buffalo Bill" Cody in 1912.

12

Duck Bill

David McCandles, in charge of the Rock Creek Stage and Express station, was a truculent North Carolinian. He was disgusted when young James Butler Hickok was assigned to the station as a stock tender. Hickok had been driving a stage for Russell, Majors and Waddell. A grizzly bear had attacked him in Raton Pass and had mauled him badly. When he recovered sufficiently to get around, he was too badly disabled to drive stage again. His left arm was almost useless, and other injuries caused him constant pain. Practically a cripple, he could do little more than painfully drag himself around. The Company had sent him to the remote stage station in Wyoming to recover.

A tall, weedy youth, with blond hair and a protruding upper lip, Hickok was soft-spoken and inoffensive. Because of his injuries he could do very little work. This annoyed McCandles, who had taken a violent dislike to him on sight. The station keeper derisively named young Hickok "Duck Bill" and harried him incessantly. When a stage pulled in and the passengers were standing around, McCandles had a habit of wrestling Hickok, supposedly in fun. The young man took it all in tight-lipped silence. There was little he could do, except quit—and where could he find another job? As the weeks passed, Hickok slowly regained his strength and the use of his mangled arm.

Although he seemed to accept his mistreatment stoically, one incident showed he was boiling beneath the surface.

He detested the derisive nickname "Duck Bill."

A Widow McCall lived near the station with her two sons, Jack, twelve, and Andy, nine. They were young hellions, as wild as Indians. One day Andy accosted Hickok with a taunting, "Howdy, Mister Duck Bill!"

Enraged, the silent, much abused stock tender grabbed a hoe and made for the boy. Andy bolted. Hickok chased him, swung the hoe and knocked his tormentor down. The boy lay still. Jack, his older brother, came running up, sank to his knees beside the boy. "Andy's dead!" he choked. The hoe dropped from Hickok's hand. He stood staring, horror-stricken.

Twelve-year old Jack came to his feet, fighting back tears. "I'll kill you for this when I grow up!"

The distracted Widow McCall strove in vain to have Hickok arrested and tried for the killing. But the whole country was in a turmoil, over slavery and the impending Civil War, and there was little law in Wyoming Territory in 1861.

The crime went unpunished.

McCandles had a wife and family at his ranch across Rock Creek. In May, he sold the station to the stage company and retired to his ranch. He still couldn't resist the temptation to goad Hickok. The Company was still paying him for the station, giving him an excuse to visit and abuse "Duck Bill." He rode in with two other men and his son, Monroe, aged twelve, and announced that he was going to "clean up."

The four dismounted at the stable. Two men, James Woods, a cousin, and Gordon, an employee, remained there. McCandles and his son walked over to the station. Mrs. Wellman, wife of the newly appointed station keeper, came to the door. McCandles demanded to see her husband. The woman told him he was away. McCandles called her a liar and said he intended to search the station. He pushed roughly past the woman—and walked into Wellman and Hickok, standing inside. Behind the two men hung a calico curtain, screening off the rear of the room.

Taken aback, McCandles stammered that he wanted a drink of water. Bucket and dipper were within reach. Hickok wordlessly dipped a drink and handed it to him. Then Hickok pushed aside the calico curtain and stepped behind it.

McCandles set down the dipper and shouted for him to come out.

"Come and get me!" called Hickok.

With an angry snort, McCandles pushed the curtain aside. A shot rang out. A bullet through his chest, McCandles staggered outside and collapsed. Woods and Gordon rushed over from the stable, while the boy leaned over his father. "Run, son, run!" the dying man gasped. The boy rushed away.

From the doorway of the station, Hickok shot Woods twice with a pistol, and his victim dropped. Gordon checked and turned to flee. Hickok fired again, mortally wounding him. He went down, and began crawling away. Hickok followed and shot him **dead**.

E. B. Hendee, the local sheriff, later arrested Hickok, Wellman, and Brink, a stock tender. They were all charged with murder. Then the Civil War broke out, and the men were released. The trial was never held.

Hickok joined the Union Army as a scout. He appeared to be a born gunman. At the battle of Pea Ridge, Arkansas, March 6 to 8, 1862, he was posted at a commanding spot for the purpose of picking off Confederate soldiers. He cut down thirty-six men.

Discharged from the Army in 1864, Hickok had trouble in Springfield, with a man named David Tutt. Tutt had sworn that he would "get" Hickok. On July 21, 1865, they met in the town square. Tutt jerked out his revolver, fired—and missed. Hickok rested his gunhand on his left arm and shot his opponent through the heart.

Hickok was now quite different from the shambling, half-crippled stock tender who had suffered the abuse of David McCandles. He was a perfect specimen of manhood, 6′ 2″, wide-shouldered and lean-waisted, with silky blond hair curling down to his shoulders. His eyes were a cold blue-gray. He wore spotless white linen, a stylish Prince Albert coat, and checked pants. A scarlet sash girded his waist. The ivory butts of twin guns protruded from holsters dangling on either side of his wide leather gunbelt. His dandified appearance cloaked cool courage.

About this time he acquired the nickname "Wild Bill." It seems that he dropped into a saloon and found it in possession of a gang of brawling toughs. They threw him out. Then the ferocity that was to mark many episodes during his life flamed. He drew both his guns and re-entered, shooting. The saloon quickly emptied. Later, when he was walking down the street, a man yelled, "Give 'em hell, Wild Bill." The tag stuck.

During 1867–8 he served as a scout for General Hancock, campaigning in Indian country. As a courier, he risked his life many times riding alone with dispatches through territory infested with hostile Indians.

Next he became a deputy United States Marshal at Fort Riley, Kansas. Always restless, he quit and appeared at Hays City, Kansas. Here he placed his name on the ballot in an election for Town Marshal.

Longhorn cattle, driven up the trails from Texas, were shipped east from Hays City. It was one of a string of notorious trail towns —Abilene, Ellsworth, Newton, Wichita, Dodge City, Caldwell— wild, lawless, where killings were commonplace and saloons and gambling houses never closed. One reporter telegraphed his editor, "Hell is now in session at Abilene."

He might have said the same of Hays City. Here long-haired drovers fresh off the Long Trail, shaggy buffalo hunters from the plains, tough troopers from nearby Fort Hays gambled, drank and fought each other with fists, knives, and guns. Sober citizens yearned for law and order, but no one could enforce it until "Wild Bill" came along.

Hickok was elected marshal. He survived where other lawmen had died because he possessed uncanny speed with a gun and seldom missed his mark. His code was to shoot first and shoot straight, and he was never careless.

He quickly gave Hays City a sample of his methods. Two drunks were wrangling in a saloon, waving their guns and threatening to shoot anyone who poked his nose into their business.

A bartender hastily sent for the new marshal.

Wild Bill sauntered in. Both drunks challenged him. He promptly shot them both and strolled out. Several lawbreakers suffered the same fate before Hickok's job came to an abrupt end.

Captain Tom Custer of the Seventh Cavalry liked his liquor. One afternoon, to show his contempt for the marshal's civilian law, he rode up and down Hays City's main street, shooting at all and sundry. Wild Bill had no option but to arrest the drunken officer and conduct him back to Fort Hays.

Sober, Captain Custer was bitter. He felt that as an Army officer he had a perfect right to do as he pleased in Hays City. He had been humiliated. After sundown, he brought five troopers to town for the avowed purpose of ending the career of Wild Bill.

They found the marshal in a saloon and piled into him. The struggling tangle of men swayed over the floor of the saloon. Although the odds were six to one, Wild Bill succeeded in freeing an arm. He grabbed one of his guns and shot a trooper. His second shot killed another. When the startled troopers drew back, three dead cavalrymen lay on the floor. Now crazed with fury, Hickok would have killed more but several patrons of the saloon jumped him from behind and held him. The ashen-faced Captain Custer and his two surviving troopers left.

General Sheridan issued orders that Hickok was to be arrested. —dead or alive. Before the cavalry patrols reached town, however, the marshal was far away. As he explained later, he couldn't fight the whole Seventh Cavalry.

Abilene was a chaos of disorder when the fugitive quietly slid into town. Mayor Joseph McCoy was at his wit's end. Tom Smith, the former marshal, had been murdered. According to *The New York Tribune,* "There is no law, no restraint in the seething caldron of vice and depravity that is Abilene."

The mayor heard of Hickok's arrival and heaved a sigh of relief. If anyone could tame Abilene, Wild Bill could.

Hickok spent most of his time gambling in the palatial "Alamo" saloon. Appointed marshal, he assigned three deputies to do his "leg work." Whenever trouble developed, one or the other hurried to him. Wild Bill did the rest. The tally of his victims at this time was reported to have reached forty.

The only man who really made Wild Bill look foolish was the outlaw, Wes Hardin. Hardin, boyish looking, blue-eyed, with a reckless grin, was one of the most cold-blooded killers in the West. When he arrived in Abilene he was dodging probably a dozen warrants for murder.

Hickok was urged to arrest him. The marshal stopped Hardin on Texas Street one afternoon, covered him and ordered him to hand over his guns. Hardin calmly pulled out his two Colt revolvers and held them out, butts foremost, a forefinger hooked around each trigger guard. Wild Bill reached for the guns. Suddenly, Hardin twirled them on the trigger guards and the marshal was staring into two black muzzles, faced with sudden death. Thus Wild Bill was introduced to the celebrated "Border shift."

Tight-lipped, he slowly slid his own gun into the holster, braced for death. To everyone's amazement, Hardin followed suit. The two dropped into a saloon to talk it over, and parted friends.

At the end of the trail season, Hickok was sitting in a rocker behind the glass-panelled doors of "The Alamo," watching a knot of drunks carousing on the street outside. One, Phil Coe, a well-known gambler, tripped over a stray dog. He shot the dog. Wild Bill charged out, a gun in each hand. Coe opened fire, and Hickok responded. One slug knocked the marshal's hat off. But two of the drunks were wounded, and a bullet had lodged in Coe's groin.

At this point, a tragedy—for Wild Bill—occurred. Mike Williams, a deputy, came rushing to his assistance. As Williams dashed up behind Hickok, the marshal whirled and fired. The deputy dropped, dead.

After this, Hickok seemed to have lost his nerve. He left Abilene and joined a Wild West show. His eyes gave him trouble. An Army doctor diagnosed the problem as glaucoma. Hickok was on his way to the Black Hills when a gang of outlaws, led by Frank Curley, an old enemy, attacked the party. Hickok had been testing his failing eyes with target practice. Only two unexpended shells remained in each gun. He promptly shot four of the bandits. Hearing his hammers click on empty shell cases, Curley moved in close to kill him. Wild Bill cheated death, as he had so often done before, by quick action. He hurled one of his empty revolvers at the outlaw, cracking his skull.

Hickok was an habitual gambler, and he was careful to sit with his back to a wall. At Deadwood, playing poker in the "Saloon 66" with three other men, he broke the rule.

On this occasion, he had stopped to talk with the bartender when he entered. When he reached the poker table the only vacant seat had its back to the saloon doorway. Hickok stood eying the empty chair uneasily.

"What's wrong?" inquired Charlie Rich, a player.

"I just don't like the location of that chair," said Hickok.

"Aw, quit being superstitious," said Rich. "Sit down and let's get started."

Hickok sat down. The cards were dealt. For a while the men played quietly. When the hands of the clock on the wall were creeping past three o'clock, a man named Buffalo Curly entered the saloon. No one paid much attention. Hickok never guessed that Buffalo Curly was the twelve-year-old Jack McCall who had sworn to revenge his brother's death many years before.

Curly stepped up behind Wild Bill's chair, snatched out a pistol, stuck it against the back of Hickok's head and squeezed the trigger. The heavy .45 killed him instantly.

The poker hand he was holding—the ace of Spades, ace of Clubs, eight of Clubs, eight of Spades—scattered over the floor. Ever after it was known throughout the West as a "Dead Man's Hand."

The murderer was hanged on March 1, 1877.

"Wild Bill" Hickok.

13

The Julesburg Episode

Old Julesburg was a cluster of unpainted shacks, huddled around the California Crossing of the South Platte River where the Overland Trail forked. One branch of the Trail angled northwest past Chimney Rock to California and Oregon; the other headed southwest through the broken hills to Pike's Peak and the Colorado mining country. Beyond Julesburg the terrain sloped up to the rocky plateaus of the Continental Divide. Worse, the five hundred or so miles of trail that meandered across South Pass to Salt Lake City was infested with warlike Sioux.

When immigrants began to flow over the Overland Trail, Julesburg grew in size and importance. Most westbound trains made the settlement a stopping place before again venturing into the wilds.

The rude settlement had grown from a trading post, founded by

Jules Beni, a French-Canadian. Jules was a big bear of a man, lawless, domineering, and unscrupulous.

Julesburg became notorious for being a hangout for desperadoes, and horse thieves—and Jules was king of them all.

Jules had suspiciously good luck recovering—for a price—teams of immigrants that had strayed. Bands of "Indians" who attacked trains near Julesburg rode shod horses. (Indian ponies never wore horseshoes.) Jules was also suspected of being involved in several stage holdups near town.

Jules was usually to be found in a bar. He received all complaints with a grin. "I am Jules," he boasted. "I am Julesburg. This is my town. I am the law." Since he was a powerful man, with several killings on his record, few argued with him.

When the Pony Express was launched it seemed a good idea to make Julesburg a "home" station, and to place Jules in charge. Very soon valuable Express ponies were reported missing. The mail was delayed. Strange stories reached the ears of Benjamin F. Ficklin, general superintendent. When his inquiries revealed that Jules headed a gang of renegades, he decided that the French-Canadian must be discharged. But Jules had let it be known that anyone sent to replace him would have a very short life indeed.

In Joseph A. Slade, Ficklin found the man he wanted. Slade was hired, appointed division superintendent and sent to Julesburg to "clean up."

Slade was no angel. It was said that at the age of twelve he killed a man by hurling a rock at him. Later, he joined the Army and fought in the Mexican War. Thereafter, he became "Captain" Slade, although there is no record that he was anything more than an enlisted man. When sober, Slade was quiet, competent, and courteous. When intoxicated he became a raging devil.

He was a "lone wolf" and a deadly shot. There was no question of his courage; he apparently never knew the meaning of fear. After the Mexican War he drove a stage, fought Indians, and ran a freight line. In Wyoming, he killed one Andrew Farrer during a drinking bout. On a drunken spree in Denver he shot up a saloon and cut down a man who tried to restrain him. The man was David Street, a stage line official, and a friend. Sobering up, Slade was bitterly repentant. He refused to leave the bedside of Street until he was on the way to recovery.

Such was the man who was sent to replace Jules Beni.

When Slade jumped off the stage and big Jules came lumbering down the rutted street of Julesburg, people ducked for cover and awaited gunplay. They were disappointed.

Jules stopped, smiled amiably and looked his successor over. "Howdy, Slade!" he said.

"*CAPTAIN* Slade, sir," returned the other courteously.

"I am Jules, I am Julesburg!"

"Wal, we better get together," said Slade. "I'm taking over the Pony Express."

"Sure, anytime you say," grinned Jules, and ambled away.

Everything went smoothly until Slade claimed several ponies that Jules swore were his. Slade insisted that they were Express Company property, and he rode out to the pasture to take them over. Jules, lying in ambush with a double-barrelled shotgun, emptied both barrels into Slade.

The hail of buckshot swept Slade out of the saddle. Apparently lifeless, he lay bleeding from a dozen wounds. Jules looked at the limp form, decided his enemy was dying and returned to town.

Later, Express Company employees found Slade. Amazingly, he was still alive. After giving him rude medical attention, they placed him on an eastbound stage.

For weeks he hovered between life and death in a St. Louis hospital. Finally, however, he recovered.

Meanwhile, Ben Ficklin, who was no "softie" either, heard of the attempted murder, and headed for Julesburg. Here he gathered a party of dependable men, cornered Jules and hanged him. But the hanging job was botched! Jules' friends cut him down. Ficklin had left town and Jules strutted down Main Street once again. Apparently the only ill-effect of his experience was a dull-red rope weal around his thick neck.

When Slade left the hospital he had but one thought: get Jules. Arriving back in Julesburg, he learned that the trapper was hiding in what is now known as Italian's Cave, a fissure in the hills about three and a half miles from town.

With friends, Slade flushed him out and cut him down with a bullet in the leg when he fled.

The wounded man was carried back to town where Slade, a cruel man intent on vengeance, killed him.

With Jules disposed of, the new Express superintendent ruthlessly waged war on horse thieves and renegades. Once he led a posse in chasing four renegades who had held up a stage. The fugitives took refuge in an isolated cabin. The ground had been cleared around it. It seemed like suicide to approach the cabin without cover. Slade told his men to remain hidden in the brush. Then he galloped up to the cabin alone, flung out of the saddle and kicked in the door. Gun in hand, he plunged inside. In the confined space, he battled four men. He killed two, and a third was mortally wounded. The survivor jumped through a window and ran. Slade rested his gun-arm on the window sill and cut him down.

But Slade was a strange mixture of ruthlessness and kindness. Once when he suspected a half-breed of horse stealing, he killed the man, burnt down his house and left the family without shelter. Then he and his wife adopted the dead man's little son, and brought him up as their own.

Needless to say, Slade's division quickly became one of the "cleanest" on the Route.

Along much of the Overland Trail there was no law, as we know it today. As Jules Beni boasted, men made their own law, and white renegades were almost as troublesome as Indians. Probably the most efficient law-enforcers were the Express superintendents and their men. Once, in midwinter, three outlaws drove off a herd of several hundred horses near Fort Laramie, including ponies belonging to the Express Company. A pursuing posse overtook the thieves in Utah. One was killed, two escaped. Shortly after, a man, footsore and half-frozen, dragged into Horse Creek, seeking refuge from the bitter cold. But Slade had given strict orders: no one, except an employee, was to be fed or sheltered in Company stations. And Slade was a dangerous man to disobey.

Moved by the man's plight, the station keeper fed him. Then the stranger dropped, exhausted, on a pile of sacks in a corner, and slept.

That day, much to the station keeper's dismay, Slade made one of his unexpected visits. The superintendent swallowed a mug of hot coffee, evidently mistook the sleeping man for a stock tender and rode on. Later, the stranger left, with profuse thanks.

The following day a stage came through. Inside was the man who had slept on the sacks, shackled hand and foot. Behind the stage rode Slade. He checked his pony and eyed the uneasy station keeper blandly. "That gent," he drawled, "was one of the hoss thieves. One was killed, another lynched in Nevada. Now we got the third." Then he rode on. The horse thief was hanged.

Yet there was one enemy that Slade couldn't overcome, and that was liquor. Sober, Slade was efficient and affable; drunk, he seemed almost insane.

Finally, he became involved in a drunken brawl in the sutler's store at Fort Halleck. Several troopers were injured and when the raging Slade was finally overpowered the place was a shambles.

The commandant served notice on the Express Company that Slade must be dismissed. Since many other complaints of his drunken escapades had been received, general superintendent Ben Ficklin decided to let him go and appointed Robert Spotswoode to succeed him. To Spotswoode fell the task of informing Slade that he had been dismissed from the Express service. Friends urged Spotswoode to take an armed guard with him. "Slade will kill you," they said.

Spotswoode chose to handle it alone. "I knew," he said later, "that if I found Slade drunk there would be trouble. I knew, too, that when sober he was the most reasonable man alive."

When Spotswoode arrived in Julesburg, Slade was out at his ranch. He and his wife welcomed the visitor and made no inquiries about his business. "Molly," said Spotswoode, "prepared an excellent meal. We sat down and ate. When we were through

I told him quietly that he had been discharged from the service and that I was appointed to take his place. Slade took it calmly and gave me every cooperation, even making up a complete inventory of Company property. He was exact about everything."

Shortly after, Slade and his wife were heard of in Colorado, where prospectors were swarming into Alder Gulch, attracted by the new gold discoveries. Virginia City and other shanty towns along the Gulch thronged with men. Riotous life blazed in dance halls, saloons and gambling joints. Daily, desperadoes murdered men for their gold dust. The sheriff of Virginia City, Henry Plummer, was the leader of the worst gang of criminals.

Vigilantes took over. Plummer and twenty of his cohorts were hanged at Bannock.

Slade had bought a ranch on the Madison River, about twelve miles from Virginia City. Saloons lured him to town. As always, drink converted him into a raging madman.

Shortly, after the hanging, Slade wrecked several saloons. The Vigilantes still held the upper hand and a Miners' Court doled out justice. Slade was arrested. He angrily defied Vigilantes' law, tore up the arrest warrant and threatened to shoot the judge.

The Vigilantes were in no mood for compromise. The Miners' Court promptly sentenced him to hang. Sober enough now, Slade pleaded for leniency. They agreed to postpone the hanging until he was able to say goodbye to his wife. A rider was dispatched across the Tobacco Root Mountains to bring her in.

Molly almost killed a horse racing to his side. When she arrived, however, her husband was dead. The impatient Vigilantes had tired of waiting.

14

Crisis

On April 12, 1861, cannon balls thudded into the walls of Fort Sumter. The Civil War had exploded. North and South were locked in a bitter struggle, which was to last for four bloodsoaked years and cost 498,332 lives.

Pony Express riders raced back and forth across the continent carrying war dispatches to half a million news-hungry citizens in California and Oregon. Butterfield's Oxbow Route had crumbled with the onset of the war. Southern sympathizers stole its horses and raided its stations. Now the "Pony" was the one slim connection between East and West.

California's gold was as vital as bullets to the embattled North—and to the South. But among the men who had migrated to the

Pacific Coast were many Southerners, and feeling ran high. There was rioting in some localities. Lacking news, California *could* have gone to the South.

But the "Pony" couriers never faltered. "Ten days from Coast to Coast," was their slogan. Month after month they lived up to it, despite hostile Indians, white renegades, and rugged trails. Many give credit to that daring string of riders for cementing California to the Union.

When the winter of 1860–61 approached many thought the Express would be abandoned. Snow blocked the Sierra passes, blizzards howled over the plains, and much of the route was a frozen waste. The San Francisco *Bulletin* said: "A few weeks are needed perhaps to settle the fact whether the Overland mail shall enter California by the shortest and most central route, or be compelled by the inclemency of winters on that route to seek a passageway by making a long circuit through a milder climate."

That same winter, figures printed in the newspaper's own columns furnished the answer. Times taken by Express riders from Fort Kearney, Nebraska, to Fort Churchill, Nevada—1,600 miles—for the month of December, were:

December	3 - 11 days	December	21 - 12 days
"	7 - 11 "	"	23 - 13 "
"	10 - 12 "	"	28 - 14 "
"	14 - 13 "	"	31 - 14 "
"	18 - 11 "		

All was well with the sturdy riders carrying the mail, but what of the men who managed the Company? Here it was a different story.

It was later claimed that Russell, Majors and Waddell was

bankrupt when it launched the Pony Express. Before another year had passed, its affairs were a tangled financial skein.

To make the reason clear we must glance backward.

Three years earlier, in 1858, Russell, Majors and Waddell had formed their partnership. Both Russell and Majors had been successful freighters, with scores of wagons on the trails, and Waddell was a prosperous banker and business man.

Together, they did an enormous freighting business. Their wagon trains travelled on the Old Santa Fe Trail, the Overland Trail, and through every frontier settlement where men needed supplies. They used over 500 big freight wagons, employed 1,700 men, and owned 7,500 freight oxen. In 1859, Horace Greeley, the famous editor, wrote of their Leavenworth depot: "Such acres of wagons! Such pyramids of extra axles! Such herds of oxen! Such regiments of drivers and other employees! No one who does not see can realize how vast a business this can be, and how immense are its outlays as well as its income. I presume that this great firm has at this hour two million dollars invested in stock, mainly oxen, mules and wagons. They last year employed 6,000 teamsters and worked 45,000 oxen."

Financially, the Company was regarded to be as solid as the Rock of Gibraltar.

A Government contract brought their first setback. This was to haul supplies for General Johnson's army, sent west to quell trouble with the Mormons in Utah. To fill the contract, Russell, Majors and Waddell had to buy a thousand new wagons and teams had to hire hundreds of men. The cost was in excess of $500,000.

Divided into forty trains, the laden wagons left Fort Leavenworth for Utah carrying 4,525,913 pounds of supplies.

Waging a "bloodless" war—Brigham Young, the Mormon leader, had ordered that no man be slain—the Mormons pestered the trains. They captured two on the Green River, cut off another on Big Sandy Creek, and scattered the oxen. Wagons carrying 300,000 pounds of supplies were burned.

General Johnson abandoned the advance and marched his army to Fort Bridger to set up winter quarters. During a heavy snowstorm, the Mormons cut out another 500 draft oxen.

At Fort Bridger the troops found only charred ruins. The Mormons had burned the fort. Supplies were unloaded on the prairie—in midwinter. Of 3,500 freight oxen, Russell, Majors and Waddell saved 200, a loss of $150,000. Wagons that had cost the Company $175 apiece were sold to the Mormons for $10—there were no oxen to haul them.

The total loss to Russell, Majors and Waddell was $642,201— $319,000 for wagons and oxen; $323,201 for freighting service. The Government agreed to pay $493,553 of this, including $72,000 for three burned trains and $84,255 for 1,906 oxen frozen or driven off.

But in fact, Russell, Majors and Waddell never collected a dollar.

Another army was sent to Utah. Russell, Majors and Waddell received a freighting contract twice as large as that of the previous year. An enormous outlay of funds was required to purchase new wagons, teams and wages. William Russell, who spent most of his time in Washington, D.C., strove to induce the Government to settle the $493,553 bill. The War Department declared that it could pay nothing without a special act of Congress. A bill to reimburse the Company was debated in both houses. Many legislators were out of sympathy with the Utah campaign. They wanted to forget the whole thing. The bill failed to pass. Russell, Majors and Waddell were called "chiseling contractors."

The Company didn't have the money to buy wagons and teams to transport military supplies under its new contract. To solve the problem, Russell suggested to the Secretary of War, John B. Floyd, that he be allowed to draw "acceptances" upon the War Department against future earnings under the contract. The Secretary agreed. Many banks advanced money against these "acceptances." Russell, Majors and Waddell went into debt for $1,731,000.

Russell was a born gambler. The "jackpot" for which he was playing was a mail contract over the Central Overland Route, 764 miles shorter than Butterfield's Oxbow Route, which received a $600,000 annual Government subsidy. By using the Pony Express to prove that he could cut Butterfield's average time in half, Russell hoped to arouse public opinion to such an extent that Congress would be forced to give him a mail contract for the Central Overland Route.

For this he had ambitious plans, which included daily coach service and a $1,000,000 a year subsidy.

Actually, the "Pony" was losing $30 for every letter it carried. Butterfield, down south, lost more. Every piece of mail cost *him* $70. The Government shouldered Butterfield's losses; Russell, Majors and Waddell carried their own.

Another load weighed down the Company, too—the Central Overland, California & Pike's Peak Express Company. Discovery of gold in Colorado in 1858 had brought a flood of prospectors. Their shanty towns were completely cut off from the outside world.

They lacked newspapers, mail service, and transportation.

The impetuous Russell decided that a stage line would coin gold.

In February, 1859, he threw in with Josh H. Jones, a freighter, and launched the Leavenworth & Pike's Peak Express. Both his partners, Majors and Waddell, objected strongly. They pointed out that the Company was already up to its ears in debt.

Russell shrugged and went ahead. On borrowed money, he and Jones built 27 stage stations, bought 50 new Concord coaches, hired 175 drivers and station hands. Total wages were $1,000 a day.

The Leavenworth & Pike's Peak Express lost money from the day it started. In ninety days, Russell's notes became due. The line was bankrupt. Majors and Waddell came to the rescue. As Russell's partner, his failure would hurt their credit. How they needed to keep that credit good! To cut losses, they bought out the Hockaday Stage Line, which ran from Missouri to Salt Lake City, for $150,000. No cash passed. Payment was in notes.

The two lines were combined under the title of Central Overland, California & Pike's Peak Express Company. It steadily lost money.

To raise money, the firm selected 3,500 of their best oxen, and drove them to California, where freight oxen brought high prices. Late in the year, the great herd moved out of Camp Floyd. It hit snowstorms in Nevada. Unable to move through the heavy drifts, 1,500 oxen died. By spring only 200 were alive. The loss was $150,000.

A new military contract for hauling freight to New Mexico brought hope to the hard-pressed Company. By going further into debt, Russell, Majors and Waddell acquired 1,500 new wagons, assembled great herds of oxen at Kansas City, built two large warehouses. Then they waited, week after week, month after month, for supplies to freight. Meanwhile they were paying an army of idle men, feeding large numbers of animals. In addition, the Pony Express and the Central Overland, California & Pike's Peak Express Company were both running at a loss.

Desperate for money, the Company borrowed every dollar it could, wages went unpaid, the Central Overland became known as "Clean Out of Cash and Poor Pay."

Russell, Majors and Waddell now owed about $1,800,000. Russell tried desperately to raise money in New York. Failing, he returned to Washington, D.C., and made a dubious deal with a minor Treasury official whereby he "borrowed" a total of $870,000 in bonds from the Indian Trust Fund. These bonds he used as security to raise money in a frantic endeavor to stave off collapse.

The Treasury official confessed. Congress launched an investigation. Russell was arrested, jailed, and released on bail. Later, the case against him was quashed by a legal quibble.

In the same month that the bond scandal broke, Congress was debating the Central Overland Mail Route. Butterfield's stages, teams, supplies, station tenders, everything movable, had been rushed north with the outbreak of war.

Russell's great gamble for a $1,000,000 mail contract had failed. Russell, Majors and Waddell sank under a load of debt. The Company was dissolved. The Central Overland was put up to public auction. Ben Holladay, who had already loaned the stage line $200,000 bought it for $100,000.

Butterfield and Wells, Fargo interests received a contract with a $1,000,000 subsidy, to carry mail over the Central Overland

Route. Stagecoach service was to be furnished six days a week, each way. The Pony Express was to be continued.

The first Central Overland stage left St. Joseph July 1, 1861, and reached San Francisco July 18.

Russell, Majors and Waddell had invested $700,000 in the "Pony." This included $100,000 for equipping the route with stations, ponies and supplies; $480,000 for maintenance; $75,000 cost of the Paiute uprising, and $45,000 miscellaneous expense. Receipts were less than $200,000.

The proud firm of Russell, Majors and Waddell, once high lord of the freighting business, had crumpled, crushed by a load of debt. Each of its partners, once reputed to be worth millions, died in near poverty.

Russell went back to New York. Where once he had been dined and wined by financiers and bankers, he was now ignored—a nobody. He entered the brokerage business, and failed. On September 10, 1872, he died at the home of a son, in Parimyea, Missouri. His age was sixty.

Majors fought to remain in the freighting business. For a while he operated on a small scale, then turned to prospecting. Buffalo Bill Cody, once one of his many thousands of employees, found him living in a shack in Denver. He was writing the story of his life, but was too destitute to have the manuscript printed. Buffalo Bill, always generous, furnished the funds. The story was published under the title of "Seventy Years on the Frontier." It brought little money. Majors died in Chicago in his 86th year.

Waddell retired to Lexington, Kentucky. One of his sons was killed defending a slave. His property was sold on the courthouse steps for taxes. Old friends spurned him. Destitute, he died at the home of his daughter, Mrs. A. G. Williams, in his 65th year.

15

The "Pony" Dies

Progress killed the Pony Express.

The immigrant's "prairie schooner" lumbered East to West in five or six months; stages of the Central Overland Mail reduced this to eighteen days; the fast riders of the Pony Express dashed across the plains in ten days.

With passing decades, railway trains made the trip in three days, and ultimately, jet planes trimmed the time to four hours.

But the telegraph flashed messages from coast to coast *in seconds*. So it happened that, in 1861, the completion of the first transcontinental telegraph doomed the "Pony."

Through the financial turmoil caused by Russell, Majors and Waddell's bankruptcy; the bond scandal that rocked Washington; the transfer to new ownership, the Pony Express had continued to operate. For twenty-four hours a day, every day, its men hurried from station to station and *mochilas* of mail crisscrossed the plains.

In August, 1860, the rate for a half-ounce letter had been reduced from $5 to $2.50. In April, 1861, it was cut to $2; on July 1, 1861, to $1.

West of Salt Lake City, Wells, Fargo now operated the "Pony." On the eastward stretch its new boss was Benjamin Holladay. Holladay was a rough, shrewd, hard-driving Kentuckian. As a young man he had been bullwhacker, muleskinner, and stage driver. During the Mexican War he had bought mules for the War Department and made enough to equip himself as a freighter. With other adventurous spirits he had headed for California. Where others dug for gold, however, Holladay sought wealth in transportation. Over the year he had built a freighting and stagecoach empire. When he took over the Pony Express, riders and station hands soon became aware that there was a hard driver at the reins.

To supervise operations, he had a special coach built, a coach fit for a king. Every appointment was regal, from silk curtains down to solid silver candlesticks. A selected team of "blooded" horses pulled this princely vehicle. In it, Holladay rocketed up and down the route.

A lavish spender, "Old Ben" was a great lover of jewelry. His fancy vests were famous. Every button was inlaid with diamonds.

Once, while his coach labored up a grade, it overtook a Pony Express rider who was "breathing" his pony. Holladay stuck his head out of the stage and bellowed, "Who owns that hoss you're straddling, son?"

"The Pony Express, I guess."

"Who owns them fancy spurs you got strapped on?"

"I do!"

"Wal, put 'em together!" thundered the boss. "Put 'em together."

The Express rider jammed home the rowells and disappeared over the rise in a cloud of dust.

Once, Holladay made a record-breaking coach trip from Sacramento to St. Joseph—1,966 miles—in twelve days, cutting six days from the regular Central Overland stage schedule.

But the days of the "Pony" were numbered.

Even before the first *mochila* was tossed over the saddle of a restive pony, a young man was writing its death warrant.

Riding a mule, he laboriously worked his way across the plains. His name was Edward Creighton and he had an idea—stringing a telegraph wire clear across the continent.

He decided it could be done.

On June 16, 1860, Congress passed an act offering an annual subsidy of $40,000 for ten years to anyone who could link East and West by telegraph. Hiram Sibley, President of the Western Union Telegraph Company, secured the contract in September, 1860. Two companies were formed to build the line. East of Salt Lake City the Overland Telegraph Company strung wire; west, it was the Pacific Telegraph Company. Edward Creighton was in charge of the eastern stretch.

The contract specified that the line had to be in operation by July 31, 1862. A frantic race ensued between the two companies to complete their allotments of line. The prize—a bonus of $50 for each day the winner beat the other to completion.

Construction proceeded at amazing speed. Here is part of Creighton's record:

August 2 - 9 . . . . 100 miles
" 10 - 19 . . . . 190 "
" 20 - Sept. 6 . . . . 225 "
Sept. 7 - 27 . . . . 250 "

Creighton's method of stringing wire was to divide each crew into three parties. One dug the post holes, the second set the poles, twenty-five to the mile, and the third strung the wire.

Each morning a ten-man hole-digging party spaced out, seventy paces apart. Each man dug a four-foot hole. When he was through he advanced seventy paces beyond the most advanced hole, and dug another. Thus the diggers worked ahead, over-lapping each other. Behind them came another six-man team. This team nailed the brackets to the poles, set them in the holes and tamped them solid. Last, a four-man team strung wire. Two additional teams were kept busy distributing poles and insulators from wagons. On the treeless prairie poles had often to be hauled 250 miles or more.

Buffalo and Indians gave some trouble. The buffalo found the poles to be ideal scratching posts. The massive beasts loosened the poles, often pushed them down. To discourage them, the poles were studded with sharp spikes. The itchy buffalo were delighted! However in a few years, they vanished from the plains.

Indians occasionally set fires around the poles and burned them down. Washakie, a Sioux chief, was persuaded to "talk" over the wire to Winnemucca, the Paiute chief in Nevada, 500 miles distant. Later, the two chiefs met and decided that their words had really been carried over the "talking wire." Thereafter, their followers treated the strand of copper with great respect.

In another case, a repair gang surprised a band of Indians busily hauling down the line. A dynamo was quickly connected to the wire. The marauders received such a jolt of electricity that they never approached a telegraph line again.

Many Indians had a superstitious dread of the strand of wire strung overhead. They feared its "magic," and would pass under it only at full gallop, crouched low across the withers of their ponies.

A transmitting station was hooked onto the end of each line. As they crept toward each other from east and west, the Express riders rushed telegrams across the rapidly closing gap. News items in California newspapers carried such notations as: "By telegraph to Fort Kearney from St. Louis, thence by Pony Express to Edwards Creek station, thence by telegraph to San Francisco."

On October 18, 1861, Creighton's crew reached Salt Lake City. He beat the western gangs by six days. His total time was four and a half months.

Brigham Young sent the first telegram from the Mormon capital to Washington, D.C.

By October 24, a strand of wire completely spanned the continent. Its completion sounded the death knell of the Pony Express. Now the telegraph carried newspaper dispatches and urgent business messages. Daily Overland stages packed letters and heavy mail.

The Pony Express was officially discontinued on October 26, 1861, and the nation, quivering beneath the impact of the Civil War, took little note of its passing. It had been in operation nineteen months, and its riders had covered over 600,000 miles. Service was only interrupted once. Only one *mochila* was ever lost.

The fast ponies that had carried the gallant couriers through dust and heat, snow and blizzard, were sold. Express riders, station keepers, stock tenders were dismissed. Some stations were absorbed by stage lines; many crumbled into decay.

Few authentic records of the "Pony" remain. Most were destroyed in a fire that swept the offices of Russell, Majors and Waddell. Not even a reliable list of the Express riders survived. But the saga of those heroes on horseback will ever light American history.

As the telegraph was stretched across the country, the Pony Express grew less and less important.

*Entries in boldface refer to captions